LIVING DANGEROUSLY
WITH THE HORN

Living Dangerously with the Horn

Thoughts on Life and Art

DAVID M. KASLOW

Birdalone Books
Bloomington, Indiana

Birdalone Books, Bloomington, Indiana, 47401
© 1996 by Birdalone Books
First edition

ISBN 0-929309-04-9

Printed on acid-free paper

ACKNOWLEDGMENTS

To Elinor, K. T., and Matthew

CONTENTS

ix

You shall no longer take things at second or third hand,
 nor look through the eyes of the dead, nor feed on
 the spectres in books,
You shall not look through my eyes either, nor take things
 from me,
You shall listen to all sides and filter them from your self.

—Walt Whitman
Song of Myself, 2

FOREWORD

IN GILBERT AND SULLIVAN'S *The Mikado,* The Lord
High Executioner gleefully reminds us that we can dispense
with "the idiot who praises, with enthusiastic tone, all centuries
but this, and every country but his own." Gilbert's commentary
notwithstanding, I am among those who lament certain aspects
of our century and country, where we often find ignorance of
physical principles, fearfulness, inattention to the dynamics of
human behavior, and the misuse of technology replacing genuine
substance and assuming lives of their own.

In the field of music-making, misused technology can hinder
our performances. For example, electronic pitch monitors have
been invented to help us develop listening skills, but ironically,
we sometimes allow our fascination with these machines to
consume the same energy necessary for gaining these skills. We
forget that listening is an active and voluntary facility, whereas
hearing is inactive and involuntary.

In non-musical life, we have devised advanced telephone
systems, electronic mail, and fax machines to enhance communication, yet at times we let our absorption with their technology
replace the actual learning of communication skills, with a resulting paucity of ability—and caring—in our everyday
communications.

xi

In the above examples, technological means replace the originally desired ends to the detriment of artistry, either musical or verbal. Ignorance, fear, and inattention have similar effects. Hornists applaud genuine progress in music education and improved musical equipment. We must question, however, the attitude toward progress which automatically equates novelty with improvement. Sometimes, as Tallulah Bankhead quipped, "there is less in this than meets the eye."

Certainly, new concepts and equipment should be considered, not simply because they are available or in vogue, but because they might help us to play more imaginatively or sensitively. For instance, we can benefit from etude books such as Gunther Schuller's *Studies for Unaccompanied Horn,* which is based on complex contemporary rhythms and harmonies. Schuller's book helps us to develop our "ear" and sense of rhythm. Of course, we also can develop our "ear" through activities apparently unrelated to our field, such as listening carefully to recorded poetry, learning the mathematical bases of the overtone series and of the relationships between notes, and studying form and color in the visual arts.

Horn players can also benefit from electronic aids such as sensitive tape recorders and the engineering accomplishments of modern instrument makers. Sensitive recording equipment enables us to analyze our playing from varied acoustical vantage points; improved instrument manufacturing techniques enable us to produce results commensurate with our efforts. Both free us to address increasingly subtle musical matters.

Musical technique is not the same as music, just as engineering is not the same as architecture, nor is information the same as wisdom. While impressive on the surface, the current pervasive obsession for playing ever faster, higher, and louder diverts much of the energy needed for learning the all-important intricacies of musical expression. When we inordinately minister to technical matters, whether as developing students or as practicing professionals, insufficient resources remain for musical elements such as style, form, and phrasing. Artistic music-making depends on the delicate interaction between musical content and the technical medium used to convey it. Certainly, insufficient technique can cause problems, but problems that are more serious than technical flaws occur when interpretation lacks emotion or intelligence. There are many lessons to be learned from master players. The most essential is always to place music foremost in importance, rather than trendiness, safety, or efficiency. (Efficiency is an appropriate goal only when its cost is likewise appropriate.) Master performers, including hornists of earlier generations such as Rudolph Puletz, Dennis Brain, John Barrows, and Bruno Jaenicke, are immersed first in music and only then in their instrument. We must be similarly occupied. Being so changes our perspective on everything we play, just as wearing sunglasses affects the color of everything we see.

I direct this book to horn players and other musicians willing to take the risks necessary for renewal, growth, and for learning to make genuine choices based on application, awareness, fearlessness, and good health, as opposed to indolence, habit, ignorance, fear, and poor health. In short, I address those willing to live dangerously with the horn.

I write as a hornist, not as a researcher, often using examples based upon my professional horn playing experiences. These examples can be readily translated by other musicians to their own disciplines, there being more commonalities than differences between even seemingly opposing viewpoints and activities. I address pre-professional horn players and offer my ideas to professionals as a "refresher course."

In addition, because many issues faced by musicians are also faced by thoughtful non-musicians, I hope that they, too, will benefit from this book. To paraphrase a Buddhist teaching, when we take one thing and learn it very deeply and carefully, we learn everything at the same time. This is primarily a book of ideas about such concepts as artistry, ego, creativity, fearlessness, relationships, and perfectionism. Some practicalities, however, such as audition-taking and health, are also addressed in depth. I discuss practicalities only when my views differ from those more commonly held, suggesting "flavors" of, rather than rules for, solutions to problems.

I intend for this book to be both source and resource, to be informative as well as a stimulus to further investigations. I do not attempt to "prove" all of my theses logically. Proofs are not always possible, since some of my ideas are based on personal and strongly held faiths, scepticisms, and experiences.

Throughout the book I imply, or address directly, the relationships between our work and ourselves. To explore this enormous subject more fully would require a separate book, and I recommend the writings of P. D. Ouspensky (begin with *In Search of the Miraculous*), J. D. Salinger (especially *Franny and Zooey*), Laurens van der Post (start with *A Mantis Carol*), and Eugen Herrigel's *Zen in the Art of Archery*, for deeper explorations of the relationships presented here, as well as of topics such as "identifying," "process and result," and "habits." The list of Recommended Additional Reading gathers these works and suggests other readings as well.

Some of the material herein requires both initial effort to understand, and further effort to personalize. Some of it is, necessarily, semantically complicated. At the risk of stodginess I will be as precise as possible in language, both to express my ideas, and to clarify commonly held but imprecise ideas which are often obscured by the murky use of words. To these ends the book perforce contains newly minted compound words and definitions devised to communicate newly minted ideas.

Brooks Tillotson, a New York freelance hornist, wrote the following to me several years ago:

It is difficult not to become totally biased to our own way, or school, of playing. We must remember the work and time we have spent developing our own playing standards. Others have done as much and more, and have as much musical and emotional right as we have to their ways. I do not think any horn player (or [other] musician) will ever upgrade his own playing by downgrading the playing of others.

I try throughout to follow the spirit of Tillotson's enlightened statement. However—and forgive the cliché—this is easier said than done. If I fail, my limitations, not my lack of convictions, are to blame. I am convinced that we reach our highest artistic goals through inquisitiveness, non-defensiveness, and intelligent openmindedness toward people, ideas, and circumstances. We reach our highest goals only when we are as anxious to explore our weaknesses as we are to find our strengths.

Two forces impelled my efforts: my love of music and of horn playing, and the not-always-gentle but always loving encouragement of the late Richard Moore, long-time Principal Hornist of the Metropolitan Opera. I acknowledge the sustenance given by colleagues and students who have accompanied me through thirty-seven years of professional horn playing and forty-one years of private horn teaching, many of whom are named within the text.

I thank the Hambidge Center for awarding a Residency Fellowship to complete this book, and the John Anson Kittredge Educational Fund, Lamont Music Associates, and the University of Denver for their assistance to the same end.

I also thank Malcolm Lynn Baker, Judy Barber, Thomas Brinton, Philip Cohen, Patricia and Richard Cope, F. Joseph Docksey III, David Dodge, William Douglas, John Ewing, Karen Gasser, Will Gravely, Aneita Gullett, Lorin Hollander, Mildred Kaplan, Elinor Kaslow, Matthew Kaslow, Donald Keats, Steven Lee, Lindy Lyman, Steven McCarl, Thomas McCoy, Paul

Mansur, Stephen Maxym, Dorrit Nesmith, Leonard Newton, Michael Oxley, Cynthia Parkinson, Johhny Pherigo, Bin Ramke, Angela Shepherd, Frances Shure, Stella's Coffee Haus, Carol Taylor, Thordis Simonsen, Richard Slavich, Melvin Wildberger, and Roy Wood. Finally, many thanks and a bouquet of freesia to Birdalone Books' publisher and editor, Viola Roth. She is a treasure.

Hornists are taught and encouraged, but are ultimately responsible for what emerges from the instrument. The same holds true for writers; I alone am responsible for any missed verbal notes or poor literary intonations.

The Hambidge Center
Rabun Gap, Georgia
September, 1994

INTRODUCTION
Paul Dunkel

A BOUT TWENTY YEARS AGO, a group of Viennese psychiatrists (who else?) released a study about stress in the workplace. Findings showed that flight controllers were the number one candidates to go bonkers because of job-related pressure. Next in line were, can you believe this...*symphonic musicians!* Now, we know that by the slip of a finger or minuscule miscalculations a flight controller can send a supersonic transport and its captive audience from here to eternity. That's pressure.

So what is it about playing in an orchestra that turns stout-hearted individuals into mental basket-cases, physical cripples, alcoholics, and worse?

The answer is: pressure—most real, some imagined.

Consider the unique plight of the orchestral musician. He is surrounded by critics.

On the podium is the biggest critic of all, who, if there were justice in life would be made to serve a minimum term as a soldier in the type of musical army he now commands.

To port and starboard, fore and aft (unless he is holding a bass drum beater), are colleagues who, at the first drop of a mute, metamorphosize into critics of the first water.

In the distance are the great unwashed. They have invested in the price of a ticket and consider themselves critically qualified to distinguish good performers and performances from bad.

And somewhere among the aforementioned horde is at least one individual who prays his name is known but begs for visual anonymity. He didn't shell out one red cent for a ticket. He is the ultimate authority, the Musical Representative of the Fifth Estate and his words, appearing a morning or two after the last chords have evaporated, are the weightiest. All the members of the orchestra hope the conductor doesn't believe a word he has written.

Finally, the worst and best critic. That would be the musician himself who, if he didn't possess the ability to self-criticize, wouldn't have an orchestral job in the first place.

David Kaslow is most interested in *this* critic because he has spent his professional career being one. As a member of several noted horn sections, as a soloist, chamber musician and as—the hardest job of all—a teacher of other musicians, he has been forced to examine his performances from several vantage points. His conclusions and suggested approaches are valuable not only to members of the brass section but to the rest of the orchestral family tree.

While most volumes directed at instrumentalists stress the physical, Kaslow's approach to the mental and spiritual aspects of preparation and performance is a breath of fresh air. Canker sores, muscle fatigue, audition trauma, "soloitis"—they are conquerable with the proper mind-set and without beta-blockers and antibiotics. Or maybe not. Kaslow opens doors that will allow each player to explore his best options.

Kaslow will be the first to admit that you won't be playing *Til* flawlessly just by reading his book. But you'll probably play it better. And have more fun doing it. Isn't that why you became a musician in the first place?

Mr. Dunkel is conductor of the Westchester Philharmonic and the American Composers Orchestra. He formerly played flute in the New York City Ballet Orchestra, and the Marlboro Festival Orchestra.

LIVING DANGEROUSLY
WITH THE HORN

A man is not an artist by virture of clever technique or brilliant methods: he is fundamentally an artist in the degree that he is able to sense and appreciate the significance of life that surrounds him, and to express that significance to the minds of others.

—Howard Pyle

I
ARTISTRY

A**RT" IS DEFINED** in *The Oxford English Dictionary* as "human skill as an agent, human workmanship."** The same volume defines "artistry" as the pursuit or occupation of an artist, and artistic characteristics and ability. To this I add that art represents, and artistry reflects, the most direct expression of the most aware self.

Artistry demands intellectual and spiritual prerequisites such as awareness, fearlessness, and application. (In these pages, "application" will mean *self*-application, rather than *other-imposed* application.) In addition, artistry contains practical components such as adherence to composers' notation, the avoidance of "hook-ups" (automatic, unwittingly made connections), and, for hornists, the proper use of air support. Prerequisite and component functions sometimes overlap; distinctions between the two are not always clear. Some aspects of artistry, such as awareness or imagination, are both. Even after our efforts to understand artistry, some of its facets must remain unexplained. Artistry is more than the sum of its prerequisites and components, just as water is more than the sum of hydrogen and oxygen; artistry is, in part, inexplicable.

Some aspects of artistry are self-reliant through self-sustaining cycles. For example, awareness is needed to generate additional awareness; passion is needed to produce more passion; application is needed to spur increased application, and so on.

Artistry is expressed in as many ways as there are people. Alas, it also can be derailed in as many ways. For instance, we are at times tempted to misuse our "other-awareness" (awareness of all that is outside ourselves) to unduly strive to please contractors, colleagues, conductors, and even those with discernment limited to "right" or "wrong" notes. Awareness, however, is always better used as a source of strength to resist such temptation, and to follow our loftiest artistic standards.

Or almost always. Possible exceptions include commercial engagements and audition-taking, both of which are "real-world" experiences where other considerations might sometimes take precedence over artistry. It is never appropriate, however, to forsake bedrock musical or ethical principles. Commercial playing is driven by commerce, not art. In commercial music-making, business, not expression, is the order of the day. Re-recording is costly, and nuances are added or subtracted in the editing booth. If an engagement is live, such as an ice show, editing usually takes place instantaneously. In these situations it is appropriate to play in a safe, inoffensive manner, and not to take chances.

Some players see this attitude as "selling out," perhaps noting that were a Dennis Brain to record a commercial jingle, he would do so in an artistic manner. True enough, but most of us are not Dennis Brain and realistically ought first, and possibly always, to put all of our energies into

Handel, Debussy, and Penderecki. Following this priority we, too, may eventually play jingles *à la* Brain. Artistry requires us to coexist with its inherent dangers and difficulties. Horn artistry demands that we take risks on behalf of our art, that we live dangerously with the horn. The dangers pale, however, beside the gratification of expressing our most aware selves through our best-crafted playing.

THE PREREQUISITES OF ARTISTRY

Awareness

A WARENESS" is popularly described as the quality and state of being informed, cognizant, sensitive, and conscious, and is sometimes used synonymously with "consciousness." I expand the definition to include being informed, cognizant, sensitive, and conscious *of ourselves*—our rational left-brained selves as well as our imaginative right-brained selves—and of all which is not ourselves. ("Mindfulness" is still another synonym for "awareness." I prefer "awareness" or "consciousness" because "mindfulness" implies awareness to be only an intellectual state.)

This expanded definition implies that what we do has unintended as well as intended effects (in medicine, the former are called "side effects"), and that everything in the universe exists in a universal context. Awareness leads to the inevitable conclusion that everything is not only connected but is ultimately the same.

Our definition of "awareness" also implies it to be both an underpinning and a component of artistry. The higher our levels of awareness, the more of the world's treasures we bring to our music-making and to our lives. As we become increasingly aware and artistic players we become increasingly aware and artistic people. With increased awareness comes an increase in the quality of our actions. Producing high-quality actions helps us to build appropriate self-confidence, which in turn promotes continued good performance. This is like our sun's energy cycle, which simultaneously consumes and, through nuclear fusion, replenishes some of its fuel. This cycle will not last forever, and eventually, the sun will die. The same applies to ourselves: we, too, eventually will run out of the life energy that Oriental medicine, science, and philosophy call *Qi*.

Artists are not merely at different levels of playing ability from other players. Rather, they are in completely different worlds from other (including good) players. Everything that artists do, whether pertaining to their art or to their everyday lives, differs from the actions of non-artists. The categories of artist and non-artist are defined by degrees of awareness: artistry requires the highest possible degree of awareness of self and of "not self."

Fully aware players would be aware of everything in the universe: every aspect of themselves (feelings, thoughts, body), everything related to music, and everything not related to music. These hypothetical, fully aware people, would not "use" every bit of awareness at every moment. Instead, their awareness would provide for their actions a network of connections to the world, which would add depth to their music-making. Of course, humans—at least ordinary ones—cannot attain full awareness. With application, however, we can achieve a high degree of awareness, providing us also with a well-developed network of connections. There are ties between awareness and theology, although the two are not identical. Increased awareness is an incidental goal of most religions, and full awareness is the primary, albeit virtually unattainable, goal of a few. A small number of people throughout human history—mainly spiritual or religious leaders such as Jesus, Mohammed, Moses, and Gautama—possibly were fully aware. While we may debate their degrees of awareness, and whether full awareness would ever be possible or even desirable, my belief is that as human beings and as musicians we should continually strive for the highest possible degree of awareness. The point is not to be "thinking" about everything in the universe at every moment; rather, it is for some part of our "beings"—our intellect or other aspect of ourselves—to be in touch, on some level, with all that makes up the universe. Whether we know it or not, whether we like it or not, the universe is always in touch with us.

We increase awareness only to the degree to which we apply ourselves to the task. This application must be constant: it is ineffectual as well as stressful to alternate focused and scattered states of awareness, like alternating focused and scattered dieting.

Many of us were taught that our best playing requires a low degree of awareness, limited to the awareness of our playing, that of our colleagues, the conductor, and, possibly the audience. On the contrary, I believe that our best playing requires the highest possible degree of general awareness: whatever we bring into the concert hall enriches and personalizes our music-making.

A high level of awareness, whether learned or innate, is essential to artistry. Hornist Bruno Jaenicke (1887–1946), composers J. S. Bach (1685–1750) and Igor Stravinsky (1882–1971), Italian tenor Enrico Caruso (1873–1921), and cellist Pablo Casals (1876–1973) must have been highly aware people. Their art communicates so much more than notes—it also communicates awareness of all areas of life.

Awareness is little valued or stressed in our culture. People who seek it do so out of inner prompting. They swim against the mainstream, often alone. Their desire for awareness impels them to find their appropriate paths. Whether traveled alone or with other seekers, all of the paths are tortuous, at first requiring visceral, and further down the road, intellectual, efforts.

For those working alone, the development of body awareness is a common visceral way to begin, because it provides a foundation for fuller outer awareness. New students of awareness often begin by gaining awareness of a body part—a thumb, for instance. By adding parts of the body to the sphere of physical awareness, the no-longer-new student gradually becomes aware of her or his entire body as a unit, rather than a group of parts. This process takes many years, but prepares students to add to their awareness all that which is outside the body. Throughout, the enemies of awareness reveal themselves to be rationalization (saying, for example, "I won't do this—it's a waste of time"), defensiveness, and habitual thought patterns, which often include free-associative thinking.

The beginning students of awareness also will be spurred in their efforts by books such as Eugen Herrigel's *Zen in the Art of Archery* (1953). In this classic East–West exposition of awareness, Herrigel uses archery as a metaphor for awareness. Any activity could have been used, since there are more similarities than differences among human activities. For horn players, the physical and spiritual principles of archery—itself a physically uncomplicated activity—can easily be transposed to the physically more complicated act of playing the horn. (Just what we need—another transposition!)

Advanced unaccompanied students of awareness—those highly aware of their bodies—can gradually add simultaneous awareness of their five senses and their breath, and, later, their increasing knowledge of the world. Knowledge is important because our various resources are too limited to allow us to discover everything and do everything. Although reading about climbing Mount Everest is pallid compared to actually climbing the mountain, reading allows us to partake somewhat in the experience.

More directly, advanced students of awareness will be inspired by *Meetings with Remarkable Men,* by George Ivanovitch Gurdjieff (1872–1949). The (possibly full) awareness of the "remarkable men" provides us with a clear goal. P. D. Ouspensky's *In Search of the Miraculous* (1949) describes exercises and "efforts" designed to increase awareness: some are spiritual, some—such as "movements"—are physical, and some are intellectual.

Guidance is also available for those who prefer to work with others. Much of it is of Eastern origin, although some systems have originated in the West. Sufism, Hinduism, Buddhism, the Gurdjieff Work, and the teachings of Krishnamurti are Eastern. Westerners such as Alan Watts (1915–1973), Robert Bly (b. 1926), Carl Jung (1875–1961), Wallace Stevens (1879–1955), and Ram Dass (b. 1931) have stressed awareness in their teachings, sometimes blending their thoughts with Eastern philosophies.

I believe that it is best to work toward awareness as a member of a group, since the encouragement and re-inforcement of a teacher and of peers is nearly mandatory. The leader should himself be in an advanced state of awareness. In *The Perfect Relationship,* Siddha self-realized master Swami Muktananda Paramahamsa (1908–1982) wrote:

> Therefore, before you set out on a pilgrimage to the Infinite, reflect upon your undertaking with great care. If you go alone, your journey will be confined to the realm of the mind. If you want to go beyond the mind, you will need a companion who has himself transcended the mind and can therefore take you by the hand and lead you on the journey. A small child needs a wise person to give him self-confidence and a helping hand, someone to kindle faith in his heart so that he can eventually stand up and walk straight on the path. Similarly, a seeker of Truth needs a strong hand and a firm support.

Gaining awareness is hard work. It is the hardest work there is. Along with its constant challenges come temporary discomforts such as those resulting from the removal of the support provided by habitual patterns of thought and behavior. This loss produces temporary spiritual or physical vacuums. These vacuums, however, become space for our true thoughts and behaviors.

Gaining awareness is also a time-consuming task. Tales of instant Enlightenment notwithstanding, most of us gain awareness slowly and by degree. We should distrust approaches to awareness promising fast progress.

We should also beware of purely intellectual approaches to awareness: as mentally stimulating as they might be, discussing awareness has very little to do with attaining it.

The intellect plays only a small role in the process, in the beginning functioning most usefully as an observer, and later as a gateway to knowledge and thence to wisdom. Intuition, instinct, and freely-flowing emotion play far greater roles than the intellect. The American novelist Henry Miller (1891–1980) reinforced the idea that it is awareness that enables humans to be most alive, and least prisoners of inner spiritual and outer material circumstances. Referring to awareness as "consciousness," he wrote:

> How to become conscious? It is very dangerous, you know. It does not mean you will have two automobiles and own your own home with a pipe organ in it. It means that you will suffer still more—that's the first thing to realize. But you won't be dead, you won't be indifferent, you won't be insensitive, you won't be alarmed and panicky, you won't be jittery, you won't throw rotten eggs because you don't understand. You will want to understand everything, even the disagreeable things. You will want to accept more and more—even what seems hostile, evil or threatening. Yes, you will become more and more like God. You won't have to answer an advertisement in the newspaper in order to find out how to talk with God. God will be with you all the time. And if I know what I'm talking about, you will listen more and talk less.

Connections

PERHAPS the most important aspect of human awareness is the recognition of interconnections and intraconnections. Awareness includes several factors: the awareness of ourselves, of that which is outside ourselves, and the relationships between the two. An eggshell illustrates all of these elements since, being semi-permeable, it is simultaneously "aware" of itself and of the outside world. The eggshell plays two opposite roles, separating its contents from the rest of the world through its *semi*-permeable shell, and connecting its contents to the world through its semi-*permeable* shell.

Jesus, Mohammed, Einstein, Moses, and Gautama, along with other leaders, realized and taught the connections in the universe which, with or without our awareness or consent, affect every moment of our lives. When teaching "love one another," Jesus emphasized connections. Even the "impersonal" sciences recognize that every action produces an equal and opposite reaction (Newton's third law of motion). No action ends with itself.

Writers and philosophers stress connections. They are a pervading motif in the works of Eastern thinkers such as Indian writers Mirabai (1498–1546?) and Rabindranth Tagore (1861–1941), Japanese writers Yukio Mishima (1925–1827) and Yasunari Kawabata (1899–1972), and Westerners such as Ralph Waldo Emerson (1803–82), William Blake (1757–1827), and Walt Whitman (1819–92). In *Leaves of Grass,* for example Whitman wrote, "Clear and sweet is my soul, and clear and sweet is all that is not my soul." The late biologist Lewis Thomas was remarkably aware of connections, and viewed ant hills as organisms composed of cells which we, with less awareness of connections, call "ants." In the *Tao Te Ching,* Lao-tzu (604?–531 B.C.), the founder of Taoism, wrote that without leaving his house he could know the whole world. Finally, from *Dark Circle of Branches* by the American writer Laura Adams Armer (1874–1963):

"Did you know," asked Na Nai, "that sounds and colors must go together? That songs and paintings must not be separated?"

"Is that more magic talk?" asked Pedro.

"It is what Uncle has taught me. He says the sound of the thunder goes with the color of lightning. The sound of the east wind goes with the white dawn, the sound of the west wind goes with the yellow of sunset. The song of the bluebird goes with the color of the day."

"I cannot understand very well," said Pedro. "I thought that a sound could go by itself."

"Nothing goes by itself. Uncle says nothing goes by itself. All things go together."

Both of the last two writers acknowledge the connections between everything that exists in the universe: Taoism is based on awareness of the "oneness" of the world; the Navajos in Armer's novel consider these connections to be part of everyday life.

On the other hand, we post-Reformation and post-Industrial Revolution beings (a.k.a. "Modern Man") often have limited our definitions of reality to what is visible and measurable, and have ignored many of the intangible realities which enrich and ennoble life. Although societal modern man subjugates itself to these limitations, individual modern man need not share these limitations. Indeed, as music-makers striving for artistry, it is imperative that we be aware of intangible realities within music-making, and of those which connect our music to the world.

The logical end result of connections is described by the contemporary American writer, Natalie Goldberg, in *Writing Down the Bones.* While discussing metaphor, she concludes that all things are not only connected to everything else, but that they *are* everything else.

> This is what metaphor is. It is not saying that an ant is like an elephant. Perhaps; both are alive. No. Metaphor is saying the ant *is* an elephant. Now, logically speaking, I know there is a difference. If you put elephants and ants before me, I believe that every time I will correctly identify the elephant and the ant. So metaphor must come from a very different place than that of the logical, intelligent mind. It comes from a place that is very courageous, willing to step out of our preconceived ways of seeing things and open so large that it can see the oneness in an ant and in an elephant.

Connections are evident on all levels of life. For instance, ordinary, limited awareness tells us only that household "garbage" is undesirable material. Ordinary, limited awareness of "garbage" is a human, and therefore imperfect, construct. Increased awareness places "garbage" in a wider perspective: while the material is unchanged (and we still remove it from our homes), we add the knowledge that garbage is first a form of matter, a universal and perfect construct, and therefore worthy of respect.

Matter consists of atoms and molecules connected to, and in relationships with, each other. Increased awareness shows us that everything, whether tangible action or object, or intangible thought or emotion—playing the horn, horses, pencils, poetry, or household garbage—is a product of the interplay of matter. Indeed, music-making can be viewed as musicians' vital energy—*Qi*—being transferred to their instruments.

Intraconnections within music-making are fairly obvious. We see them among instruments, all of which follow physical laws governing the behavior of tangible materials such as brass, membranes, and strings. We see them among composers: Beethoven and Brahms were masters of the symphonic form. Interconnections between musical and other paradigms are less obvious but just as real. For example, music and physics are interconnected through the overtone series, the laws of which determine the notes that can be produced on a given instrument, whether "in tune" or not. The overtone series, in tandem with laws governing resultant tones, determines the proper tuning of chords. Finally, the laws of the overtone series have an impact on musical form, determining modulations within movements as well as key relationships between movements.

Principles of music and of politics are also interconnected: the dialogue of negotiation is similar to the dialogue within a fugue. Also, we can see interconnections between music and language, where words are like notes, synonyms are like timbres of instruments, sentences are like phrases, punctuation markings are like cadences, and so on. Connections can provide music teachers with analogies, similes, metaphors, and new vocabularies. These tools, however, should be restricted to students with sufficient breadth to cross between disciplines.

Application

HORNISTS know firsthand that attaining or maintaining artistry requires application, which is hard work, and includes practicing, studying, thinking, and analyzing. Although artistry's hard work is fatiguing, the fact that it is being directed toward something we love makes it also energizing—again, like the sun, simultaneously burning and replenishing fuel.

Application is most effective in the context of a high degree of awareness. Without awareness, application is often directed toward inappropriate goals, or is scattered, Sancho Panza-like. The late University of Chicago Professor of English and novelist Norman Maclean saw that "Power comes not from power everywhere, but from knowing where to put it on." He made this observation in his first novel, *A River Runs Through It,* while describing casting technique with a fly-fishing rod. Confirming Maclean's observation closer to home, we see that the highest possible attainments for hornists are achieved by players who, through application, build their resources (using awareness of opportunities, including "bad experiences," for growth), conserve their resources (using awareness of physical, emotional, and intellectual energies), and who marshal their resources (using awareness of the nature of their assigned tasks). These are the players who know "where to put it on."

Applying ourselves is not only difficult, it is dangerous. It can lead to disappointment for goal-oriented people who may not always realize their outer goals, and produce frustration in process-oriented people who may not always realize their inner goals. Whatever our orientation to goals, we must apply ourselves and live with the risks inherent in caring about anything—we must live dangerously with the horn. I like what the great jazz trumpet player Miles Davis (1926–1991) said about risk-taking: "Do not fear mistakes. There are none." To this I add that there are no mistakes only when we apply our most highly developed selves to our tasks. We are born with *de facto* and potential abilities and awarenesses, all of which we are responsible for using and developing to the utmost. When we bring our best selves to our music-making, we accomplish all that we can. Then, there are no "mistakes."

Passion

CONTEMPORARY American essayist and novelist Annie Dillard described the "flavor" of passion when she wrote, "One of the things I know about writing is this: spend it all, shoot it, play it, lose it, all, right away, every time." Aware of the connections between the disciplines of writing and horn playing, we can consider passion to be equally necessary for artistic music-making.

We need passion to overcome the illogicalities of music making: there is little that is logical or calculating about partaking in so difficult an activity. There is even less that is logical or calculating about doing so as a profession. Passion provides the energy to "challenge and transcend the constraints of logic," as described in this paragraph from *In the Lake of the Moon,* a novel by David L. Lindsey:

> Swain was smart, but he was not smart enough, and he lacked the one essential ingredient that would make him a truly dangerous obstacle: passion. Cold calculation would lose to passion every time; it simply wasn't capable of generating the heat that was necessary to challenge and transcend the constraints of logic. Barcena understood the liberating potential of passion.

Passion drives the spirit with which we make music: it impels us to apply ourselves fully to every note, whether it is part of a performance, rehearsal, lesson, or practice session. Passion also makes us realize that there is not time to waste. Given our limited resources of energy and life span, we must sustain passion throughout our music-making years. As the English wit Quentin Crisp (b. 1908) observed, "It's no good running a pig farm for thirty years while saying, 'I was meant to be a ballet dancer.' By that time, pigs are your style." Pig farming is incompatible with horn playing as well as with ballet dancing. While we cannot approach all of our activities and relationships with the highest degree of passion, we must approach at least our art in this manner.

Imagination

ALBERT EINSTEIN said that, "Imagination is more important than knowledge." Although imagination might be considered to be knowledge in an intangible form, Einstein's observation nevertheless does make an important point. For music-makers, immersed as we are in abstractions, imagination performs a vitally important function of translating abstract concepts such as grace, passion, and timbre, into tangible sounds. For those of us seeking artistry, imagination wears two hats: it is both a prerequisite for, and a component of, artistry.

I prefer the term "imagination" to "creativity" for two reasons. First, because all "things" in the universe were created by the Big Bang, ever since that cataclysmic event "things" have only been re-created. These "things" include *Crime and Punishment, The Rite of Spring,* monkeys, the theory of Relativity, bananas, and man. Saint Augustine of Hippo (354–430) wrote that the only miracle is Creation. We, our activities, and our "things" are part of the miracle of creation. We can only imagine and re-arrange within this miracle.

Second, the word "creativity" is often misapplied, referring to actions that manipulatively draw attention to their perpetrators; many a huckster has been called "creative." Passively receiving attention as a result of merit is qualitatively different from actively seeking attention by manipulating people or circumstances.

The distinctions between creation and imagination are not merely semantic. Remembering them helps us to retain a sense of awe for our universe, and produces in us healthy humility. This humility need not cause us to feel insignificant. Although indeed we are specks in an unfathomably large universe, we are at the same time parts of an unfathomably large miracle.

We are all imaginative, although to varying degrees. Most of us are aware of lettuce, garlic, olive oil, croutons, eggs, salt, lemon juice, Worcestershire sauce, Parmesan cheese, and pepper. But few of us, like Caesar Cardini, have sufficient imagination to have invented Caesar Salad.

Some musicians, such as cellist Pablo Casals, oboist Bruno Labate, and hornists Dennis Brain and Bruno Jaenicke, were incomprehensibly imaginative. Still, they did not "create." Rather, they took the materials surrounding them—surrounding all of us—and imaginatively refashioned them. Similarly, there are compositions which are so imaginative that it is difficult to understand the process by which they were conceived. I consider Johannes Brahms' First Symphony, J. S. Bach's *Goldberg Variations,* and Igor Stravinsky's *The Rite of Spring* to be such works.

"Art is exactitude winged by imagination," wrote the German–Swiss Surrealist painter Paul Klee (1879–1940). Imagination, along with awareness, application, and passion, is a prerequisite for artistry. In concert with artistry's aforementioned inexplicable aspects, these factors can produce artistry—if also we attend to practicalities.

THE COMPONENTS OF ARTISTRY: SOME PRACTICALITIES

Accuracy

As I NOTED in the Foreword, the most important musical practicality is placing the music first in importance. The foundation of so doing is to play composers' exact notations. The printed page contains many notations aside from pitches. We must communicate them all: stylistic indications, dynamic markings, rhythms, tempi, and articulations. Following these notations both acknowledges composers as the true authors of our music-making, and brings their artistic presence to our performances.

Composers notate musical imagination and we must follow their maps. Even with the freedom to interpret composers' markings—as in Baroque improvisation, Classical embellishments, Romantic *rubato*, and twentieth-century aleatory—we first must communicate the composers' intentions as conveyed by their notations. For music-makers, notations are like shoes: once we put them on we may walk wherever we wish, within the confines of historical practices.

Of course, in ensemble playing we have less freedom of

fit into a conductor's overall conception of the composition. It would be short-sighted, self-indulgent, and irresponsible to play every note exactly as we wished. Nevertheless, even in ensemble playing there is room for self-expression; few conductors demand absolute submersion in their plan.

Historical Style

PLAYING in the correct historical style is another important practicality. Only with historical perspective can we accurately communicate composers' intentions. For example, history informs us that in the Classical period, phrases often are of uniform length and balanced with one another, and that in the Romantic era, phrases often are irregular in length and overlapped. History often also tells us the appropriate tone quality, dynamics, articulation, and tempi for a given composition. Our understanding of historical style also provides an added dimension to our sight-reading skills: knowledge of the idiosyncrasies of the various epochs and of their composers enables us to anticipate sequences, chord progressions, and modulations. Because music of the late twentieth century is often so eclectic, we must sometimes depend on composers' written introductions to explain the structure and style of their compositions.

After we understand historical styles intellectually, we can practice communicating them tangibly by composing a passage and practicing it in various styles. Another form of this exercise is to play an existing passage in various styles, but without changing any of the original notations. For example, we might play a passage of a Brahms symphony in the Baroque or Classical style by changing only timbre, phrasing, and interpretation of articulations.

Air Support

A IR SUPPORT is the key technical element of horn playing. Containing the same potential energy we find in a tightened mainspring of a watch or a stretched rubber band, air support helps us to convey the emotional and intellectual expression typically and best communicated through art.

For a hornist, wind player, or singer, optimum air support consists of (1) taking the fullest possible breath, whether or not we plan to use all of it, and (2) employing the breath appropriately, with sensitivity to all of the air column's aspects that operate in tandem, such as quantity, compression, and velocity. These aspects will be discussed later in this chapter.

Air support affects all of the technical properties of playing, including endurance and regulation of dynamic level. Most importantly, however, optimum air support makes possible fine, characteristic, tone quality.

Among its many imperatives, artistry requires us to play every note as beautifully as possible, no matter what its context. To do so, we first must be able to regulate the air to the greatest degree possible. This, in turn, necessitates our taking the fullest possible breaths every time: we best manipulate the air column with full lungs and maximum involvement of the upper torso in driving the air column. As we shall see later in the chapter, the "extra" air (that is, the air not directly used) provided by full breaths plays an important foundational role, similar to that played by the "extra" knowledge (i.e., not directly used in our daily lives) acquired through a liberal arts education.

Many fine texts address air support, and some of these are mentioned in the list of Recommended Additional Reading. We must beware, however, that in many otherwise excellent texts the term "air support" is sometimes used in a limited sense, referring only to *quantity* of air, ignoring the several other aspects of the concept mentioned here. This limited usage renders the phrase nearly meaningless— similar to describing what we are wearing as "clothes," or what we are eating as "food." In reading about air support, then, we ought first strive to understand the writers' particular interpretation, and then to compare that with our own definition: the fullest possible breath, and the appropriate use of all aspects of the air column.

Tone Quality

W E MUST provide the largest possible quantity of support appropriate to every note, remembering that quantity of air *support* is not necessarily the same as quantity of *air*. As already discussed, an abundance of potential energy—air support—yields the finest and most characteristic horn tone.

Characteristic horn tone, like fine string tone, tends to contain surface buzzes and rasps, that do not "carry." There is the danger that we might attempt to refine the tone so much as to forfeit its essential characteristics, a danger that we also can observe in other areas. For instance, commercial food processors, preoccupied with long shelf-life, sometimes overly refine their products, destroying their essence. We must be careful to avoid "throwing the baby out with the bath water."

In *The Teachings of Don Juan: A Yaqui Way of Knowledge,* Mexican-American mystic Carlos Castaneda (b. 1931) wrote:

> For me there is only the traveling on paths that have a heart, on any path that may have a heart. There I travel, and the only worthwhile challenge for me is to traverse its full length. And there I travel—looking, looking, breathlessly.

Castaneda's concept of the "path with a heart" as it applies to us as hornists consists of the deciphering of and following our unique personalities as people, musicians, and hornists. These personalities tend to express themselves through the horn's noblest characteristic: its tone. Our tone ought to accurately reflect us as people and as musicians. Without this dimension, even a "good" tone is, in a sense, an inappropriate tone.

We ought not to expect the "path with a heart" always to follow an efficient, straight line. Often, it describes an inefficient, rather circuitous route. A "path with a heart" does not always coincide with a "path of least resistance," which I define as a path followed without awareness, application, or well-developed technical skills.

Not surprisingly, the "path of least resistance" for hornists leads to imitative, less-than-unique tone quality. Of course, this does not mean that we should not seriously consider the ideas and the deeds of other players, and even emulate them at times, to the best of our abilities. We must always, however, filter these ideas and deeds through our most aware selves.

The "path of least resistance" can produce, among other detriments, an obsession with a picture-perfect, "breakless" embouchure. This attitude diverts attention from what is a legitimate obsession—the production of unique and beautiful tone—and causes us to stray from the "path with a heart." Of course, some horn players have naturally "breakless" embouchures. On the rare occasions when these embouchures also produce a fine sound, the "path with a heart" and the "path of least resistance" coincide. Most of us, however, cannot develop a breakless embouchure also capable of producing beautiful sound. If this is the case, we ought not to strive for a breakless embouchure.

An embouchure that only increases efficiency pays homage to efficiency rather than to music. Efficiency, while useful—at times, even essential—always comes with a price tag: in the case of the horn player, the bill is paid through less-than-optimum tone. The price we gladly pay in another area of life may well be inappropriate to pay in our horn playing.

A beautiful musical line requires movement from the most resonant part of a note to the same part of the next. This movement frequently produces breaks in the embouchure with which, given sufficient practice, we can become comfortable. Players seeking beautiful tone often allow breaks in their embouchure, realizing that air, not the lips, produces their tone, and that their embouchure regulates, but is not, the air—just as a faucet regulates, but is not, the water.

It simply is illogical to follow the "path of least resistance" to the detriment of tone quality. In the words of bank robber Willie Sutton, we ought to "go where the money is." For hornists, a large portion of "the money" is tone quality.

Dynamics and Range

ARTISTIC USE of dynamics is an important practicality in musical communication. Just as verbal content must be conveyed at an appropriate dynamic level (we do not whisper when we are angry, nor shout when we feel tenderly), musical content must be conveyed at an appropriate level. Examining the physical aspects of playing that determine dynamic levels provides us with an opportunity to observe the interplay among several aspects of support: quantity, compression, and velocity. These aspects operate in tandem, since no single factor of the air can effect (although it does *affect*) a result we seek.

Quantity of air has already been discussed as the general foundation for all that we do with the air column. Specifically, air quantity plays a role in producing both dynamic levels and the large range of notes of the horn: soft notes require a smaller quantity of air per unit of time than do loud ones, high notes require a smaller quantity of air per unit of time than do low notes. No matter what the dynamic level, long notes will, of course, consume more air than do short ones.

Air compression is produced by the controlled contraction of the abdominal and back muscles. Air compression, like air quantity, plays a part in producing both dynamic levels and the large range of notes available on the horn. Soft notes require a higher degree of compression than do loud ones; high notes require a higher degree of compression than do low notes. Adjustments in both air quantity and compression must constantly be made, based upon the amount of air support needed for a particular range and dynamic.

Velocity is simply the speed at which the air is driven through the instrument, and its most important role is in the production of dynamic levels. Soft playing requires slowly-moving air and loud playing requires quickly-moving air. Using air velocity to regulate dynamic levels assures the production of a consistent tone quality throughout the range of the horn.

Another valid, quite spiritual viewpoint was explained to me by the late, eloquent hornist Rudolph Puletz, who from 1937 to 1941 was Principal Horn of the Cleveland Orchestra under Arthur Rodzinski. He believed that to play beautifully one must take a big breath, send it to the heart, and only then send it to the lips.

Endurance

THE ABILITY to play well for long periods of time, or to play well while fatigued (the two are not necessarily the same), enables us to digest the occasional "feasts" that are part of the well-known "feast or famine" cycle. The most effective use of air, awareness and sensible husbanding of resources of energy, and a well-developed and properly used embouchure, produce the maximum ability to endure.

There are at least two ways to build endurance. The first is straightforward and easily attainable: we can learn to endure through enduring. The musculature of the face, hands, and torso can be strengthened through sensible, prolonged use—remembering that overusing muscles (beyond "sensible") is destructive to muscle tissue of the face and upper torso.

The second way also is straightforward in concept but difficult to attain: becoming what may be called an "unmoved center," a stable being that applies its energy only where needed while keeping the rest of itself in repose. For musicians, this means using only the parts of the body, mind, and heart that are actively involved in music-making, while keeping the rest of the body "unmoved."

The parts of our bodies that remain "unmoved" while playing are not unaware, or "asleep." On the contrary, although they are not directly involved in horn playing, they enrich our playing by supporting the parts of the body that are actively involved. This is analogous with the "extra" air that we do not directly use, but which provides support for the air that we do use, and the "extra" knowledge, to which we earlier alluded, gained from a liberal arts education, that we do not directly use, but which provides bases for other knowledge that we do use.

Becoming an "unmoved center" requires qualities such as awareness, fearlessness, good health, and an understanding of the natures of "control," relationships, and perfectionism. These are the main subjects of this book.

Avoiding Hook-ups

ANOTHER practicality to which I earlier alluded is the avoidance of automatic, unwittingly made connections between unrelated aspects of playing, such as linking loudness with the high register, the highest note of a passage with the climax of a phrase, or a crescendo with repeated notes. I will call these inappropriate linkages "hook-ups."

Hook-ups differ from natural inter- and intra-connections. Whereas the latter result from immutable universal laws, hook-ups result from human imperfections, such as automatic physical and intellectual responses.

Rather than be guided by automatic responses, we must play by design: tempi should be those that we choose, dynamic levels should be those that we choose, articulations should be those that we choose, and so on. It is almost always undesirable to behave automatically. The possible exceptions are automatic habitual behaviors we have chosen to keep, and of which we retain awareness. Two examples of this are (1) our daily warm-up routines—part of an habitual action that we do not "choose" daily, yet that we must execute with as much awareness as possible, and (2) our usual physical position for horn playing, that, again, we do not "choose" on a daily basis, yet of which we must retain awareness. In both of these cases, we benefit by not having to "reinvent the wheel" every day, while also benefitting from awareness—being able to react spontaneously to unusual circumstances.

Note that the word "automatic," as used above, refers only to *acquired* automatic responses, such as defensiveness—which arises from the need to show that we are correct, rather than to see the possibilities for learning that are inherent in being incorrect. We usually learn automatic responses from parents, teachers, or other authority figures. The danger is that often these responses do not communicate our truest selves.

There also are innate automatic responses with which we were born. These responses were necessary for self-preservation during infancy and early childhood. Certain fears, such as of falling or of being abandoned, were beneficial to us as children, but as adults they are of debatable usefulness. The debate lies in the belief of some people that innate responses represent our true selves and therefore ought to be retained, whereas others believe that innate responses represent our immature selves and therefore are inappropriate in adulthood.

I believe that innate automatic responses ought to be considered to be starting points, to be understood intellectually and viscerally. If they are consistent with awareness and artistry they should be kept. Otherwise, they should be discarded.

Automatic behavior does not permit the genuine choices (again, those based on factors such as application, awareness, fearlessness, and good health) inherent in artistry. When we "choose" X because we fear Y, because society prefers X, because X is more easily accomplished, because X is our habitual response, or because we are ignorant of Y, we do not genuinely choose—we merely act as passive agents of happenstance.

Technique and Musicality

BOTH players and teachers usually find it best to approach technique within the context of musical expression, and to consider both of them concurrently, and to be almost inseparable. We should remember that we slur, trill, or play staccato so that we or our students may produce music, not perform in a circus act. Of course, it may be useful to separate musicianship from technique temporarily so that we may focus on one or the other, but the two should be rejoined by the end of a playing session.

Those of us who are teachers should present high musical values in accessible forms to avoid frustrating young students. We should stress to our students the importance of learning from all other musicians, as well as from non-musicians. When appropriate, we can draw parallels from other fields: phrasing can be learned from writers, organizational skills from businesspeople, physical training from athletes. All activities have aspects analogous to horn playing. Our demands must, however, be realistic. Young students simply have not had the life experiences essential for a high degree of artistry. Most of them have not yet experienced romantic love, deep disappointments, or the death of a loved one, all of which will expand their range of emotional responses. Nor have they experienced the cycle of failure and transcendence over failure which will encourage them to take the risks necessary for artistry. We should teach the loftiest musical values in the first lesson—not later, as incidental material. It becomes increasingly difficult to add musical values as time passes. I recently finished work with a professional hornist in a fine orchestra who initially described himself as an excellent technician but a poor musician—he thought that he "played like a hack," and I could not disagree with this assessment. As we worked, he not surprisingly found it necessary to increase his awareness of phrasing, form, tone color, harmony, and fine points of intonation. He had to redefine his playing and himself. He also had to make surprising changes in his posture, equipment, and even dress (looser, to accommodate the fuller breaths now necessary to produce his new conception of tone). In many respects he became a "beginner" again. Had his crucial, all-important early musical education been different, so, too, would have been his later circumstances.

Both players and teachers must also stress the lifelong spiritual, emotional, and intellectual growth and renewal necessary to promote artistic growth. We should reassure our students whenever growth and renewal place temporary obstacles before them. Reassurance might spare our students the fate of the hypothetical centipede who, while learning which leg moves first, becomes temporarily unable to move at all.

New or misapplied knowledge can make any of us what is frequently (and incorrectly) called "self-conscious." As the term is often used, "self-conscious" means the opposite of what surely is a desirable state—consciousness *of self.* Knowledge, however, even when it is inappropriately applied, remains preferable to ignorance, because knowledge contains seeds of growth and renewal.

Growth and renewal are not merely "the icing on the cake." They are the cake. They keep our playing fresh, and communicate our current emotional and intellectual realities. Furthermore, hornists who do not renew themselves or grow will, in all likelihood, neither take pleasure in making music nor enjoy a rewarding career.

Problem Solving

THERE ARE at least three effective approaches to solving problems: (1) using native abilities, instincts, and intuitions, (2) intellectually analyzing a problem, and (3) attempting to imitate others. After using one approach, it is best to re-solve problems using the other two, since one successful solution is not always sufficient. This gives us the fullest possible view of problems and their solutions. Sometimes, alternative solutions prove essential for musicians, just as they sometimes do for pilots who occasionally rely on their instruments instead of their senses for guidance.

In the interest of efficacy, our initial approach to solving problems should be carefully chosen. Some problems yield more easily to one approach than to another. For instance, many players most quickly improve their tone by more effectively using their native abilities and instincts, rather than by intellectually analyzing sound-production, or by imitating other players. I repeat, however, that after reaching one successful solution it is best to re-solve this, or any, problem from other viewpoints.

The third approach—imitating others—provides short-cuts to goals, although we cannot, nor would we wish to, completely imitate another musician. We can and should, with clear conscience, use the work of others as springboards to improving our own work, provided that we do so with awareness, and within the context of well-developed technical skills. As we discussed earlier, imitation must not be an unaware, default, or lazy approach to achieving goals. The American poet Alan Dugan teaches his students to master their influences, and novelist Ray Bradbury reassures us that, "Your passion will protect you from slanting or imitation beyond the allowable learning-point."

Even with successful problem solving, few of us excel in all aspects of playing. Common sense suggests, however, that we must try to develop them all to our maximum potential. For most players, this will be sufficient to both relish playing the horn and to enjoy a satisfying career.

In addition, there are exceptional players who never quite master technique, but compensate through exceedingly fine musicianship; there are as many ways of achieving artistry as there are musicians. "Truth is a circumstance, not a spot," observes Harvard evolutionist Stephen Jay Gould. Artistry—a form of truth—is likewise a circumstance, not a spot.

When I was a young boy, I attended a recital by a renowned horn player. I arrived at the performance confused, having been warned by my teacher that this person typically missed many notes. I assumed that if this were so, the mistakes would spoil the performance. (I also wondered why the well-known player was well-known.) Indeed, he did miss many notes, but I was nevertheless moved by his performance. I was fortunate to have had this experience because it increased my awareness of the possibilities within music-making.

Most of us cannot play as well as this player. Compared to him, we are dependent on correct notes to convey our musical messages. When we focus primarily on musical content, however, we almost always communicate them— even when our technique fails us. Besides, it simply is more sensible to put our energies into the joyful act of making music, rather than into the stressful act of avoiding technical failure.

Technique is certainly important. Correct notes, true pitches, and accurate dynamics are the primary conduits of our musical messages. Furthermore, "technical" societies such as ours demand it. Most of us, however, do not have unlimited resources with which to perfect both our musical and technical skills, and so these resources must be carefully allocated.

Francisco Donaruma, an erstwhile fellow horn student at the Manhattan School of Music, taught me that while we cannot completely avoid technical inaccuracies, we can always avoid musical inaccuracies. To the degree we ignore musical content, we produce, at best, "circus acts" (technically good but musically empty performances) or, at worst, "vacuums" (musically and technically poor performances).

To avoid circus acts, it is helpful to practice music in which mistakes are inevitable. For example, we can strive to play the solo part of the Tchaikovsky Violin Concerto expressively, despite mistakes. We thus learn to overcome our reliance on correct notes to communicate musical messages. As a bonus, we also learn not to be "thrown" by errors.

In orchestral playing, instances abound in which musicianship solves or eases technical traps. Let us look at two examples that illustrate this: Siegfried's "horn call" from *Die Götterdämmerung* by Richard Wagner, and the well-known (albeit not well-loved), rapid, ascending passage in Antonín Dvořák's *Carnival Overture*.

The main trap in the Wagner excerpt is neither its high tessitura nor its exposed nature. Instead, the challenge is to hear the first and second notes of the passage (concert F♮ and C♮), to be played after hearing five beats of C♯s and F♯s in the orchestra. The concert F and C effect an abrupt modulation of a tritone, from B Major to F Major. Identifying and becoming aware of the abrupt, problematic modulation can be achieved through intellectual analysis of the score. Solving the problem then can be accomplished, at least initially, either by using native musicianship or by imitating the musicianship of others—for instance, by listening to recordings.

The Dvořák passage is a fast, ascending E Minor diminished seventh arpeggiated chord, played in octaves by the first and second horns. It is often seen only as a technically difficult passage to be "gotten through." While it is indeed difficult, playing it is simplified if first we are aware of the structure and purpose of the chord, and then concentrate on communicating Dvořák's intellect and emotions through it. This communication can take place even amid a few missed notes.

Intensity

A S WE discussed earlier, music may be understood simply as energy. Sometimes music demands energy in a highly intense state, sometimes at a low level of intensity. No matter what its level, intensity can be either static, producing frustrating and confining feelings of restraint, or it can be varied, producing the excitement inherent in change.

Musicians—both composers and players—often communicate intensity through dynamic levels. Factors of pitch and timbre remaining the same, loudness is usually more intense than softness. For dynamic levels to most effectively convey intensity, the largest range appropriate for a composition should be used. Of course, there are exceptions, such as the muted *Adagio for Strings* of Samuel Barber, and the funeral piece in Edvard Grieg's *Peer Gynt*. As these works illustrate, dynamic levels are not the only mechanism for varying the levels of intensity. Others include tempo and rhythm (the time elements of music), pitch, under- and overstatement, timbre, accents, *rubato, tempo,* vibrato, and note length. In addition, we can alter the directionality of the sound. Pointing the bell away from the body produces a direct, bright, intense, clear tone suited to music of the Baroque and Classical periods. Pointing the bell toward the body or into our clothing yields a non-directional, warm, dark, and diffused tone appropriate for music of the Romantic period.

No matter how it is produced, intensity changes over time and distance in a concert hall: *forte* becomes *piano* and *piano* becomes inaudible, and a slightly bright sound becomes dark. We must exaggerate levels of intensity to accommodate the well-known "man in the last row of the balcony."

Of the many conveyors of intensity, we will next examine two which are underemployed: the time elements of tempo and rhythm, and under- and overstatement.

TEMPO AND RHYTHM

Steady tempo is the determinant from which intensity can be conveyed through the time elements of music. We can strengthen this foundation through practice with a metronome. Steady tempo is also the foundation of rhythmic accuracy. Every rhythm contains an inherent intensity level that can be conveyed only if the rhythm is played accurately. To do so, we must subdivide the beats of a steady tempo, using the largest appropriate note value: it is unnecessary, for example, to subdivide into sixteenth notes when eighth notes would suffice.

Steady tempo also is the foundation of another intensity-producing mechanism: playing at the beginning (the front) of a steady beat to communicate high intensity, and playing at the end (the back) of the beat to produce low intensity. This works because there is latitude within a beat; we can vary where we play within the beat, while at the same time keeping the outward beat steady. This latitude is distinct from changing the actual placement of the beats, as in the modern concept of *rubato* (that is, *accelerando* or *ritardando*).

The tempo of music (that is, the speed of the repeated beat as opposed to the latitude within each beat) frequently corresponds to the level of intensity of music: most often, the slower the tempo the higher the intensity, and the faster the music the lower the intensity. The *Adagio for Strings* exemplifies the former, Hector Berlioz's *Roman Carnival Overture* the latter. I must emphasize, however, that these generalities do not always hold true. As we avoid all hook-ups, so, too, should we avoid inadvertently linking intensity level with mood: high intensity might convey joy, sorrow, or any of the emotions in between. Other hook-ups derived from intensity that we should avoid include tying tempo with mood (since any tempo may be used to communicate any emotion), and linking mode with mood (since either major or minor mode may convey any mood). As with the interrelationships within the air column, intensity is a product of several factors working together.

When we are able to keep a steady tempo and to play with rhythmic accuracy, we can genuinely choose the strictness or the spontaneity that flourishes only within discipline. Lacking discipline, the "free interpretation" of tempo, rhythm, or of any component of music, is not expressive, but merely sloppy.

UNDER- AND OVERSTATEMENT

Understatement is a powerful tool, achieving subtle, sophisticated, and long-lasting effects on many psychological and sensory levels. For understatement to communicate intensity successfully, close attention by both performer and listener is required. Overstatement, on the other hand, is a less powerful tool, achieving obvious, earthy, visceral effects that are usually limited to the sensory level. Any aspect of music can be under- or overstated.

Performers today traditionally understate the music of the Baroque and Classical eras, and overstate the Romantic. It is not possible to generalize about the music of our century, because many modern techniques, including polytonality, serial writing, and aleatoric composition require new approaches to the compositions in which they are used. But even the traditions of Baroque, Classical, and Romantic music are not definitive; tradition is not law. For example, we might occasionally understate overly "romantic" Romantic music such as that of Mahler and Tchaikovsky. Conversely, we might overstate nearly-Romantic Classical compositions such as Beethoven's *Eroica,* or Schubert's "Great" C-Major Symphony.

Strong intensity through overstatement is common. An example is Beethoven's setting of the word "Gott" in the last movement of his Ninth Symphony, on a loud, sustained, implied F Major chord in the key of A Major. This chord, built on the lowered submediant of A Major, is very dramatic, although, like much overstatement, its effect dissipates quickly. Overstatement often demonstrates the proverb, "more is less."

Paradoxically, high intensity can be achieved through understatement. Claude Debussy provides us with an example of this in the fourth scene of act 4 of *Pelléas et Mélisande.* Mélisande sings *"Je t'aime aussi,"* at perhaps the most powerful moment in the opera, in the most understated manner: softly, on repeated middle Cs, in unaccompanied recitative style, and with inactive rhythm. These factors together generate high intensity through inactivity.

Under- and overstatement can also be observed in other areas. In humor, for example, understatement is the mechanism of satire, whereas overstatement is the driving force of parody. The first mechanism is demonstrated by Ogden Nash (1902–1971), in his understated gem of three words:

Purity
Is obscurity.

Overstatement may be illustrated by the anonymous "It takes a big man to cry, but it takes a bigger one to laugh at him." As in music, understatement is more powerful in humor than overstatement. The understated Nash makes us laugh longer and deeper than the overstated "big man" joke.

Nature eschews uniformity and favors diversity; she abhors monocultures. This principle explains the recurring "weeds" we find in grass lawns. It is behind the small amount of female hormones in the bloodstreams of men, and of male hormones in the bloodstreams of women. In a similar vein (so to speak), we find neither under- nor over-statement in a pure form: each contains elements of the other.

"Art Does Not Come Easy"

HORN ARTISTRY requires us to confront challenges. Some are intrinsic to horn playing, whereas others are self-generated through ignorance, fear, defensiveness, or inertia. These challenges are similar whether we seek artistry in horn playing, house building, pool shooting, or fly-fishing. Norman Maclean describes these challenges and the rewards of overcoming them:

My father was very sure about certain matters pertaining
to the universe. To him, all good things—trout as well as
eternal salvation—come by grace and grace comes by art
and art does not come easy.

Overcoming the challenges that ensure that "art does not
come easy" exposes us to permanent and temporary frus-
trations and failures as we adopt new thoughts and actions.
A typical challenge is to learn how to attend to both praise
and criticism.

There are two types of praise, and two kinds of
criticism: skilled and unskilled. Skilled praise and criticism
are conferred by knowledgeable and sensitive listeners,
whose opinions are based on discernment of, for example,
historical accuracy. Unskilled praise and criticism are
bestowed by unknowledgeable and insensitive listeners,
whose opinions are based on superficialities such as
"pyrotechnical" feats of skill and technique. If we are aware
of this we avoid being seduced by unskilled praise or
devastated by unskilled criticism. When we learn to
recognize these responses for what they are, we can then
instinctively and straightforwardly ignore them.

Dealing with skilled criticism, however, is a subtle
process. Skilled criticism can be helpful, but only if it is
understood within its specific circumstances. On the other
hand, even skilled praise has very little place in musical
discourse. Praise is virtually unnecessary to highly aware
players. They know what is positive and what is negative,
and have little need for reinforcement of the positive.
Furthermore, praise is disrespectful to the art of music:
praise ignores music while it aggrandizes either the
relationship between the praiser and the praised, the opinion

of the praiser, or the "false" ego (to be discussed in Chapter Two) of the performer.

Experiencing music as an art is different from experiencing it as personalities engaged in its performance. Arnold Schoenberg recognized this when he forbade applause at concerts of his *Gesellschaft für Privataufführungen* (Society for Private Performances).

Choosing a Course

THE DECISION of a course to take is best based upon hard-won awareness, skill, and fearlessness. Despite the emotional and psychological dangers of traveling this path—it is dangerous as well as unsettling to relinquish habitual ways of thinking and being—this pathway is the road to artistry. We become predisposed to choose this course if we remember that when we practice our art with an overriding concern for music, inner and outer success tends to come, unsought and gracefully integrated into our musical and extra-musical lives.

Staying this course requires growth, including analyzing ourselves, music, and the world. The course also demands sacrifices such as practicing, purchasing expensive instruments, paying for instruction, and studying myriad subjects. By so doing, however, we transcend the constraints of unawareness, "false ego," fear, ignorance, and indolence. Then, as artists, we are prepared to soar:

> And there is a Catskill eagle in some souls that can alike dive down into the blackest gorges, and soar out of them again and become invisible in the sunny spaces. And even if he forever flies within the gorge, that gorge is in the mountains; so that even in his lowest swoop the mountain eagle is still higher than the other birds upon the plain, even though they soar.
>
> —Herman Melville, *Moby-Dick*

Chance favors the prepared mind.

—Louis Pasteur

II
FEARLESSNESS

THIS CHAPTER addresses material for which there are neither resolutions nor absolute answers. I therefore present it not as dogma, but as serious considerations of complicated subjects. I hope that my thoughts will impel readers to distill their own conclusions. We will first look at fear, courage, and fearlessness, then more closely at fearlessness itself, and, finally, at how these behaviors affect the taking of auditions—a real-life and often fear-provoking necessity.

FEAR

SOME HORNISTS fearlessly jump into the dangers and difficulties that the horn has in store. Others persevere despite fears. While I do not completely understand motivation–my name is Kaslow, not Maslow[*]—I nevertheless believe it useful to ponder "fearlessness," which is a stance held by the most successful horn players.

Fearlessness is, of course, not limited to horn playing. For example, in *Young Men and Fire,* Norman Maclean wrote, "It is very important to a lot of people to make un-

[*]Abraham H. Maslow (1908-1970), American psychologist and philosopher best known for his self-actualization theory of psychology.

43

mistakably clear to themselves and to the universe that they love the universe but are not intimidated by it and will not be shaken by it, no matter what it has in store." Maclean was describing "Smokejumpers"—young men (and now, young women) who parachute into remote forest areas to fight fires—and his book is a chronicle of fearlessness.

The *Oxford English Dictionary's* definition of "fear" is a good starting point: "the emotion of pain or uneasiness caused by the sense of impending danger, or by the prospect of some possible evil." Fear is a perennial problem, an emotion that can be crippling, even lethal.

Many fears are of common types, and may be acquired early in life, in adolescence, and in adulthood. They often are intentionally or unintentionally conveyed by parents, teachers, and other authority figures. A horn player's scenario of a common early-acquired fear might be an authority figure (perhaps a teacher) communicating his or her fear of a passage, and the horn player's subsequent fear of the passage—even before attempting to play it. Fear-provoking situations are, of course, individually defined. Some people find fear in situations in which others take delight, such as riding a roller coaster, or playing a difficult passage of music.

Fear may be either innate or acquired, and may be in response to either concrete or imagined dangers. Innate fears tend to be found in young people, and the response to imagined dangers that they elicit is exemplified by surreal nightmares. Innate fears responding to concrete dangers, such as falling, are the grasp reflex and the startle reflex found in infants.

There are at least three kinds of acquired fear, each a response to its own type of danger or difficulty. The first is an acquired fear of a concrete difficulty. An example is the fear—learned either through experience or through others —of playing a large, exposed slur, or of making a soft, high entrance. As a shorthand, I will call this "concrete fear."

The second kind is an acquired response to an imagined danger or difficulty. This often results in psychological problems, such as a poor self-image, fear of failure, fear of success, need for approval, and agoraphobia (the fear of being in public—literally, "fear of open spaces"). Such fear often arises from responses that were useful at one time but are now outdated, such as the fear of parental abandonment. This kind of fear is often more devastating than concrete fear. I will name this "imagined fear."

Imagined fear and concrete fear may be present together in a single circumstance, producing a third kind of fear. For example, in playing the "long call" from Wagner's *Siegfried* we may fear both its concrete difficulties and the possibility of failure. I will call these combined fears simply "fear." (Amid this sea of nomenclature, remember that labels are most useful when describing extreme situations, and least useful in "gray areas." Labels are not the same as that which they represent—they are merely verbal approximations.)

Whatever its basis, fear is unnecessary. Despite concrete fear's basis in real danger, it can be eliminated by solving— through study and practice—the problem that is causing it. Imagined fear is also unnecessary, and can be eliminated by removing—through study or psychotherapy—the problem that is causing it. I do not wish to seem callous or flippant about the difficulties surrounding the discarding of fear. I acknowledge that this is one of the most difficult tasks we can face.

It is difficult to learn to play a soft, high note or a large slur; it is difficult to overcome a psychological problem such as a poor self-image. But these and other difficulties can be overcome. We need not be resigned to fearfulness provided that we are willing to apply ourselves to problems and to obtain the aid of others when necessary.

Some fears, we should note, are temporarily useful catalysts: they stimulate the flow of adrenaline, elevate the pulse, and increase the rate of breathing, thus enhancing our activity levels. To be useful, however, fears must be short-lived and produce an immediate, constructive response. For example, out of fear of committing a musical error we are moved to increase our knowledge about music. Out of fear of technical shortcomings we are moved to practice. Out of fear of the unknown we are moved to seek new experiences, or to revisit old ones in new ways. In revisiting old experiences, however, it is essential that we bring "freshness"—new skills, new spiritual or psychological insights, or simply openness—to enable us to re-encounter an experience without preconceived expectations. Merely repeating old experiences is not the same as having new ones.

Although fear is unnecessary, fearless respect for a difficult task is appropriate: we cannot play well if we are lackadaisical. Indeed, every action we perform must be given the energy, focus, and high level of awareness that are its due. We must acknowledge that fear produces real feelings and real physical responses. Fear should be taken seriously, even as we work to rid ourselves of it. Fear felt by our students also should be acknowledged, even while we help them to overcome it.

Many fears originate from negativity toward ourselves, others, or toward the universe. Such fears cause us to apply our energies only to *our* problems, and to see our problems as the center of the universe. Fears isolate us and prevent our connecting with the rest of the world. They diminish us. In the 1986 movie, *Desert Bloom,* the observation is made that, "A girl who's all wrapped up in herself makes a pretty small package."

Fear saps and diffuses psychological energy, causes tension, and blocks self-confidence. Its physical effects include shallow breathing, memory loss, "cotton mouth," and trembling. The physical cycle produced by fear destroys air technique, a tool which could prevent fear, as the AIDS virus destroys the very cells that could prevent the disease's entrenchment. Fear may be likened to the various memory functions of a computer. It is as real as the images on a screen, but also as transitory. As images can be deleted from a computer screen, so also can fear be deleted from our lives, and well it ought to be, because it drains vitality and joy from music-making.

Finally, fear confuses our understanding of true ego. We often misuse the word "ego" by defining it as "power-seeking," "arrogance," "insecurity," "fear," or "defensiveness." For instance, we might describe a braggart or show-off as "egotistical." In such a case, however, we are observing "false" ego.

In the Western sense, true ego (or simply "ego") is the awareness of, and comfort with, all of the strands of our being. These "strands" were what G. I. Gurdjieff, the twentieth-century Russian philosopher and mystic, called our "inner voices," often resulting in a cacophony with which our bodies, intellects, intuitions, instincts, and spirits must vie for our attention. The contemporary South African writer Laurens van der Post poetically calls these voices our "tappings." To an Easterner, ego is that which blocks recognition of the connections between ourselves and the universe, and with a deity. It is this lack of awareness, and the ensuing feeling of isolation, which leads to fearfulness.

Ego, in the Western sense, is the source of our best work. It is not our enemy. It helps us to grow in awareness, fearlessness, easily-flowing emotion, knowledge, skill, security and—by helping us to reunite with the energy of the Big Bang—to achieve "near-perfectionism," as will be discussed in Chapter Five. Ego precludes the desire and need to seek attention, and teaches us the difference between eccentricity for its own sake and honest, individual differences. Truly egotistical people are highly aware and fearless. They have no need for "courage."

COURAGE

A COMPOSITE dictionary definition of "courage" would surely include the ideas of acting in spite of fear, and of using courage to overpower fear. On the surface, courage seems to be a positive trait; it is, however, a waste of energy. Because fear is unnecessary, so, too, is courage. At best, courage is only *temporarily* useful as we work toward fearlessness.

We should note that courage and fearlessness are different traits. Fearlessness is, by definition, the absence of fear. On the other hand, courage acknowledges the presence of fear, lives in a symbiotic relationship with it, and implies a willingness to overcome the same fear repeatedly. By legitimizing courage and fear, we perpetuate both.

Furthermore, courage wastes resources, being analogous to cutting a finger and then bandaging the cut, rather than avoiding the cut.

Players using "courage" (in itself undesirable) to enable them to perform the *Siegfried* "long call," for instance, follow cumbersome paths, paved with misused or inappropriate behaviors, including the achievement of "courage" through will power. While will power is a positive trait, it is misused when employed to overcome fears which it would be more advantageous to eliminate altogether.

Among these inappropriate efforts to gain courage is the use of excessive mouthpiece pressure. Although inordinate mouthpiece pressure does help, in the short term, to reduce unevenness in horn tone and to play notes in the high register, it also reduces the ability of the lips to vibrate and restricts the blood supply to the lips, thus inhibiting the tone and hastening fatigue by increasing lactic acid build-up in the lip tissue. Perhaps more undesirable is the failure to address problems of tone and range which could—with application—be solved.

Another, and controversial, effort to gain courage is through the use of drugs such as anti-depressants, relaxants, beta-blockers, and alcohol. Many players have strong opinions about the propriety of taking drugs, and although it is open to question, most of us agree that some of them (for instance, propranolol, a commonly used beta-blocker which temporarily suppresses feelings of fear) can be, in a limited sense, effective. I believe that decisions about whether to resort to taking drugs ought to be individual, but that they must be reached within contexts of self- and other-awarenesses: awareness of our bodies and minds, and of the drugs' possible side effects, including their possible abilities to produce physical or psychological addictions. When drugs are deemed appropriate, they should be used with caution, under medical supervision, for as short a period as possible, and they must not be considered substitutes for attempts to solve underlying problems. In the end, we should remember that the courage produced by these drugs is itself of limited value.

Courageous approaches simply are too cumbersome, too circuitous, to generate the best possible performance. Courage only temporarily empowers us, and at potentially great cost. It is senseless to legitimize courage by legitimizing fear. We should limit ourselves to confronting only the real, unavoidable problems in horn playing.

FEARLESSNESS

FEARLESSNESS is composed of a high degree of awareness, an understanding of "control," and the belief in the benevolence of both ourselves and of the universe, of which we are a part. These three attributes together take us beyond mere courage and increasingly into the area of fearlessness.

There are several ingredients in addition to the belief in the goodness of the universe, including our ability to trust ourselves, others, and nature; our knowledge of self; our maintenance of a non-defensive posture; our strong ego; and our understanding of the nature of "truth." Belief in the goodness of the universe helps us to gain awareness, and is itself a product of awareness. This belief is more easily maintained if we remember that every event is benevolent to someone or something: the rain that spoils our picnic is good for the plants. In *Shambhala: The Sacred Path of the Warrior,* the Tibetan teacher Chogyam Trungpa (1939–1987) writes:

> It is not just an arbitrary idea that the world is good, but it is good because we can experience its goodness. We can experience our world as healthy and straightforward, direct and real, because our basic nature is to go along with the goodness of situations. The human potential for intelligence and dignity is attuned to experiencing the brilliance of the bright blue sky, the freshness of green fields, and the beauty of the trees and mountains. We have an actual connection to reality that can wake us up and make us feel basically, fundamentally good. Shambhala vision is tuning in to our ability to wake ourselves up and recognize that goodness can happen to us. In fact, it is happening already.

Belief in the benevolence of the universe most certainly does not nullify our responsibility to behave in the best possible manner. On the contrary, being part of a benevolent universe confers upon us the responsibility to take joy from the benevolence that surrounds us, and to strengthen our individual benevolence. This belief is not necessarily religious in nature. Rather, it is simply the realization that we can directly experience, and work within, the world that we inhabit.

Knowing the goodness of our world, we see our shortcomings as only temporary. Knowing the goodness of ourselves, we see the futility of falseness both toward ourselves and toward others. We then live steadfastly within our present truths, and are simultaneously open-minded to the discovery of new ones.

In Eastern cultures, a loosely defined combination of awareness and fearlessness is often called "fierceness." As bellicose as this word seems, it connotes the focused energy and high degree of awareness solely within which— ironically perhaps—peace thrives. This same focused energy is discernible in a beautifully played note, causing the note to sound alive. (This is not caused by vibrato, since the focused energy comes from within the note, not the player.)

A small number of people seem to have been born fearless. Most people who become fearless do so in stages. The first stage is fear*ful*ness, the second courageousness, and the final stage is fear*less*ness. Fearlessness is not the same as ignorance. Fearlessness is a mature stance gained by study, thought, and applied spiritual underpinnings. Ignorance is an elementary state retained due to unawareness, thoughtlessness, and a paucity of spirituality.

We have the broadest focus on our work when we are fearless. We do not manufacture false musical or psycho- logical difficulties, but instead address only innate difficulties. Fearless, we are free to engage joyfully in music-making; when we are fearful, we use so much energy overcoming fear that we are deprived of this joy.

Fearlessness helps to fuel artistry. For example, a fearless approach to the *Siegfried* "long call" takes us beyond the instrument. We might, for example, com- municate Siegfried's personality as revealed in the call, or we might focus on the call's universal symbolism. Using the combined energies of fearlessness and a high level of awareness, we place the "call" in a larger perspective.

Fearlessness is hampered when we let others others define "success" for us. The New York free-lance hornist

Brooks Tillotson addressed the nature of both fear and success in a 1989 letter to me:

> Nervousness comes in and out of one's playing experience like so many unwelcome guests crashing a party. It is truly an outside experience trying to get in. Worst one of all is "approval" fear, definitely an outside influence.... The player must concentrate keenly upon his musical equipment...and must be honest to himself and to no one else.

We should define success for ourselves within a context of ego, fearlessness, intelligence, openness, and skill. Only such a context is conducive to growth.

Sometimes we use platitudes such as "Just take a big breath," or "Just ignore the audience," in our attempts to overpower or obscure fear, rather than to remove it. These bromides, like drugs, are temporary "solutions" which ignore or mask real problems. Temporary solutions most often come from outside sources, whereas permanent solutions generally arise from within. At best, temporary solutions produce courage, that is itself of limited value. They do not produce fearlessness, and may also result in dependencies and other problems of their own. Perhaps most sadly, temporary solutions weaken our inner resources, rendering us less able to cope with future problems, and leaving us with a concomitant loss of "control."

Control

WE OFTEN think of fearless players as those who "control" their playing, and we devote much of our practice time to achieving such "control." This search reveals a paradox, however: although absolute control does not exist—perhaps no control exists—we must behave as though it does. If we wish to grow, yet we do not know for certain how much we actually can control and direct our growth, we must behave as if our actions *do* matter, thus ensuring that we make our best efforts toward growth.

This paradox is parallel to that encountered in the process of living and learning. To live effectively, we must have beliefs upon which we act, despite the questionable accuracy of human perceptions and knowledge. Aware "living and learning" behavior is based on our perceptions of truth, with the simultaneous realization that these perceptions might be incorrect. At the other end of the spectrum is unaware and prejudicial human behavior that, while also based on perceptions of truth, does not recognize the possibility of error. When regarding human perceptions and knowledge, we should remember that the world was flat until the fifteenth century, that water always flowed downhill until we discovered that it flows uphill as it approaches absolute zero degrees, and that Jeremiah Clarke's "Trumpet Voluntary" used to be composed by Henry Purcell.

Perhaps control does not exist: witness the proverb, "Life is what happens to us while we are making other plans." We carefully prepare so that we may control a performance, then become ill the day of the concert. We buy a fine instrument so that we may control our tone, then the instrument is stolen. During our practice, we meticulously learn to control the phrasing of a passage, then find that the conductor asks for a different one.

One can indeed see life as a series of inevitabilities. When we retrospectively analyze any event we see the circumstances that, with seeming inevitability, led to its occurrence. This is an old idea, Roman emperor Marcus Aurelius (A.D. 121–180) having made this point in his *Meditations.* It is not surprising that we might conclude that we partially, or even completely, lack total control of our destinies. Each of us has to come to terms with the issue of control. Without control, our lives become more spontaneous, and perhaps more dangerous. Henry Thoreau's understandings of spontaneity and control were reflected in his journal: "A man's life should be as fresh as a river. It should be the same channel, but with a new water every instant." Spontaneity is expressed by "new water every instant," and control by "the same channel."

No matter what our individual conclusions, we must behave as though some control were possible: to govern our lives as if every moment were preordained would remove incentive to seek awareness, and to reflect upon and improve our actions and our inner selves. (Alan W. Watts addresses this in *The Wisdom of Insecurity.*) While it is arrogant to believe that we can have complete control over anything (perhaps "influence" is a better word), let us also remember that, "chaos theory" notwithstanding, careful preparations in everyday life most often yield predictable results: we remain healthy, our Alexander is not stolen, and the conductor appreciates our musical instincts. Stan Getz said, "I never play a note I don't mean," showing that playing can seem controllable—at least for Stan Getz! (Incidentally, Newtonian physics is quite compatible with "chaos theory": "chaotic" events are determinate, although unpredictable by man.)

In pondering control, we should remember that it is easier to deal with issues while they are still possibilities, rather than after they are already realities. For example, it is easier (by practicing) to deal with the possibility of playing a passage poorly than (by explanation or crawling into a hole) to deal with the reality of having played a passage poorly.

Even seemingly achievable control can sometimes be an obstacle to artistic music-making, however, when it blocks spontaneity. We play our best when we attempt to control that which we can and ought to control. We play our worst when we attempt to control the uncontrollable, or that which ought not to be controlled. Ironically, the fear of loss of control can become a self-fulfilling cycle, like the drunkard in Antoine de Saint-Exupéry's *The Little Prince,* who drinks to forget he is a drunkard.

Accepting the nature of control helps us to achieve a realistic balance between playing with control and playing with abandon. The appropriate balance differs from person to person, but there will be times (for instance, when concert hall conditions are different from those anticipated, or there is a last-minute change of conductor) during which we must gracefully "abandon the driver's seat." In addition, we should remember that fear and surprise have many aspects in common: both appear to have an uncertain outcome, and both cause us to feel out of control. As we remove surprise, we remove fear.

To play—or to live—beautifully we need balance between strength (the result of a high degree of awareness, caring, application, predictability, and skill), and vulnerability (the result of abandon and spontaneity). In *Sacred Clowns,* Tony Hillerman illustrates this balance of strength and vulnerability that he has observed in the Navajos, whose strength lies in their wisdom of embracing the inevitability of life's problems. Their vulnerability lies in that they are, as are we all, entirely subject to these and similar problems.

> The way he understood hozho [the Navajo metaphysical concept of the harmony of nature] was hard to put into words. "I'll use an example. Terrible drought, crops dead, sheep dying. Spring dried out. No water. The Hopi, or the Christian, maybe the Moslem, they pray for rain. The Navajo has the proper ceremony done to restore himself to harmony with the drought. You see what I mean. The system is designed to recognize what's beyond human power to change, and then to change the human's attitude to be content with the inevitable."

As we try to understand "control," we also must remember, like the Navajos, that caring about something does not necessarily mean controlling it. In *A River Runs Through It,* Norman Maclean illustrates this principle while describing his father's fishing rod: "It was wrapped with red and blue silk thread, and the wrappings were carefully spaced to make the delicate rod powerful but not so stiff it could not tremble." The father's caring about the rod is evident in his admiration of its power and its beauty. On the other hand, the father's ease with his inability to control the rod absolutely is evident in his acceptance of the necessity for the rod to tremble.

When we (the many non-Navajos and non-fishermen among us) judiciously exercise control, we can somewhat control our journeys, expressing individual versions of the Navajo's strength or the fishing rod's "power." If at the same time we relinquish control, expressing our vulnerability or "trembling," control itself ceases to be an issue, and our actions are natural, spiritual, strong, beautiful, and grounded in truth. We are both strong and vulnerable, able to care and able to relinquish control: we are at ease with the ambiguities of "control."

Fearlessness, *Qi* (the life force), Nature, Spirit, Strength, and Beauty, are interchangeable verities, and facets of, or different names for, the ultimate diamond: Truth. Many great minds and spirits allude to this in various ways. The three examples that follow can strengthen our resolve to bring truth—all that is true, as well as all that could be true—to our music.

> Beauty is truth, truth beauty—that is all ye know on earth, and all ye need to know.
>
> —John Keats, *Ode on a Grecian Urn*

> In case the world was devastated...then nature would still begin to breed new life again, begin to push forward again with all the fine and strong forces inherent in matter...These forces, which are "inextinguishable," I have tried to represent.
>
> —Carl Nielsen, on his "Inextinguishable" Symphony

> An equation for me has no meaning unless it expresses a thought of God.
>
> —Srinivasa Ramanujan, Indian mathematician

Keats equated beauty with truth; Nielsen believed that "inextinguishable" nature represented endurability, an often-assumed aspect of truth; Ramanujan held that a thought of God is equivalent to mathematical truth. As we try to understand and to incorporate control into our lives, we must value and nurture truth as one of its important components.

Paths Toward Fearlessness

WHEREAS the most serious study of ourselves and of our interconnections to the world would be optimum, some of us choose popular, less time-consuming, and less complex paths toward fearlessness that try to maximize the possibilities within the way we already are. Others of us choose deeper approaches that profoundly *change* the way we are.

Among the popular meditational and philosophical approaches to fearlessness are the practice of Transcendental Meditation and books such as Eloise Ristad's *A Soprano on Her Head; Why Man Takes Chances* (edited by Samuel Z. Klausner); and Claude M. Bristol's *The Magic of Believing*. (The last was a favorite of Philip Farkas.) We will soon examine some of the deeper approaches to fearlessness.

As we have seen, fears can arise during any stage of life, and can persist throughout a lifetime. Some players retain debilitating fears that were formed early on, such as poor self-image, self-destructive personality, blocked emotional paths, fear of failure (or of success), and agoraphobia, and are so debilitated by these or other core problems that they cannot function at all. Such players must confront these problems, using strong traditional or non-traditional therapies. (Indeed, even players with minor problems often benefit from these therapies.)

The powerful psychotherapies of Freud, Jung, Maslow, and others are those most commonly used in our Western society. There also are systems that combine facets of several of these types of therapy. Of course, not all therapists are equally skilled, nor is any single method of therapy appropriate for every person: it is essential that a productive unit be formed by patient and therapist. Jerome Frank's classic, *Persuasion and Healing*, provides much information on the various schools of psychotherapy. Undergoing any kind of psychotherapy may be a difficult, frustrating, embarrassing, and painful experience. In addition, it demands a large commitment of energy, money, and time: Jungian or Freudian analysis can take many years. For those needing psychotherapy, however— people who cannot find solutions within themselves or with the help of their friends—its costs are small compared to the costs of not undertaking it.

Less commonly, non-traditional spiritual programs like the Gurdjieff Work, or Shambhala Training are undertaken. The Work, formally established in France in 1922, is composed of the study of Gurdjieff's eclectic view of the universe (containing Christian and Buddhist influences), exercises to increase self-observance, visceral (i.e., nonintellectual) exercises such as dance "movements," and weekly "tasks." All of these efforts share the goal of increasing our self-awareness, and, later, our awareness of all that is outside ourselves. Gurdjieff describes becoming aware as "awakening." In the Work, much attention is given to observing the habits and other automatic responses that underlie (and undermine) much of what we do, and that result in our "sleeping" through life.

The Work is a difficult undertaking. While it is often effective, it is so intense that it should be undertaken only by people sufficiently stable to withstand its psychological demands and its appetite for stamina. Suitability of new students should be jointly decided between the prospective student and the teacher. P. D. Ouspensky's *In Search of the*

Miraculous (cited earlier) is an excellent introduction to, but not a substitute for, the Work.

The Work continues to be the greatest challenge in my life—even greater than playing the horn. My long-standing involvement in the discipline, from 1955 until the present, both as a group member and as an individual, has affected me in many ways, some ineffable and some tangible. Before describing a few of the tangible ways in which I have benefitted from the Work, I must emphasize that most of them are, for me, of a fleeting nature. When I say "centered", I mean that I sometimes am centered; when I say "present", I mean that I sometimes am present.

The Work has helped me to increase my autonomy (we will discuss autonomy in Chapter Four) by helping me to clarify my physical, intuitional, intellectual, and emotional inner voices. This has made it possible for me to enter into relationships in which I am aware of and retain my uniqueness, while I simultaneously give freely to the relationship. (We will address these "composite" relationships in Chapter Four.) In helping me to become increasingly autonomous, the Work has made me more "centered" within myself—more aware of my intellect, emotions, intuitions, and energy—and simultaneously more "centered" with, and increasingly fearless of, the universe. In addition, the Work has helped me to understand and to be present in "the moment"—the instant that is composed of all that is true or potentially true, tangible or intangible, at any time. Gurdjieff's teachings have shown and reminded me—much to my horror—that pre-packaged responses, such as automatically acquired and unawarely obeyed habits, rob me of my life energy and of my involvement in the present. This awareness has enabled me to discard many of my formerly habitual responses. Furthermore, I have learned to see myself and my life in an expanded context. The world does not revolve around my sore throat, pay raise, or the note I missed last week. Rather, the world *includes* my sore throat, pay raise, *and* missed note.

The Work has produced several tangible effects in my life as a musician. For instance, through becoming more autonomous and centered, I have been able to define my own playing, and thus have become prepared to play in horn sections in which I am allowed to play as I wish, the other players are allowed to play as they wish, and together we expect to produce a section that we all desire. Also, the Work has shown me the importance of not "identifying with" my playing: neither my best playing nor my worst playing is my totality. Instead, both my best and my worst playing merely represent a part, a momentary truth, of my completeness.

The knowledge that is revealed through Gurdjieff's Work can, of course, be discovered through other studies. Shambhala Training, for instance, is based on ancient Tibetan, Indian, Chinese, Japanese, and Korean teachings that were gathered by Chogyam Trungpa, and was first taught formally in 1976. The training consists of five levels, each including sitting meditation, classes, discussions, and individualized work with a teacher. Components of fearlessness, including purposefully acquired and awarely executed habits, general goodness, and renunciations of negative states of mind, are examined. Besides instilling fearlessness, Shambhala Training seeks to augment other characteristics, such as awareness, gentleness, positiveness, and the unity of body and mind, all of which are relevant both to artistic horn playing and to everyday life. Like the

Gurdjieff Work, Shambhala Training is a serious undertaking. Trungpa's book, *Shambhala: The Sacred Path of the Warrior,* provides an explanation of the course, but cannot substitute for personal experience of the studies.

As we navigate past the obstacles on the road to awareness and fearlessness we ought constantly to recognize that music-making is, at heart, a joyful activity. The French call music *le jeu de notes* (the game of notes). It is for this *jeu* that we are musicians. While we must, with utmost seriousness, remove any obstacles to experiencing this joy, let us also remember Farkas' statement in *The Art of French Horn Playing*: "Remind yourself occasionally that your work comes under the heading of entertainment. You are not about to perform an operation in which someone's life will be at stake."

Taking Orchestral Auditions

WHETHER we are fearless (highly aware) or fearful (relatively unaware), there are many ways to prepare for and conduct ourselves at a symphony audition—the kind most of us take. The remainder of this chapter is devoted to these techniques.

Like many activities, an audition can be approached grudgingly and stintingly—as mere business—or as an activity worthy of the investment of our best resources, including intelligence, perseverance, sensitivity, and ethical grounding. Given its importance to our careers, we ought to considser an audition to be worthy of our best efforts.

Before we begin, I wish to make two points for those who are new to this daunting necessity. First, we must be "maniacal" about every audition; we must temporarily "live for" it; we must direct all of our energies toward it. Whether we do this or not, someone else will. Apropos of this, an observation was made after Super Bowl XIV (1980), in which the Pittsburgh Steelers defeated the Los Angeles Rams: "The Rams came here to play, but the Steelers came here to win. The outcome was never in doubt." Of course, the interesting situations are those where both teams—or several auditioners—"come to win."

Second, novice audition-takers must be certain that they are at a level, both musically and technically, to play a credible audition, even if they do not realistically expect to win the position. For serious professionals, or those aspiring to that level, there should be no "throw-away" auditions. A poorly played audition might well forestall future employment with the same or other orchestras, or with the conductor hearing the audition. Conductors often recall or keep files on auditioners and discuss the pool of available players with each other.

An audition cannot be fear-provoking to a fearless person. Most of us, however, are not yet fearless. As Henry Allen wrote in *Newsday* in 1990, "We may very well have nothing to fear but fear itself, but we do have fear itself."

While we do indeed have "fear itself"—that is, until we become genuinely fearless—I recommend adopting, throughout the chronology of the audition process, the physical and psychological façade that results from the following "fierce" posture: we are granting a favor to the audition committee by auditioning. The "fierce" façade also serves the larger purpose of helping us to change our inner "posture" through the mechanism of changing our outer posture. (This same mechanism can be observed when we relax our bodies and notice that our inner posture concurrently relaxes itself.) Of course, when we achieve fearlessness, the façade of "fierceness" is no longer a façade. Our purpose at an audition is to "get the job." It is not, necessarily, to "play well" according to the usual meaning these words convey. At an audition, the odds are against convincing the conductor or committee that our way of playing a passage is better than theirs. We should therefore play in the manner that we know will please the conductor and audition committee, provided that so doing does not conflict with our fundamental ethical or musical principles. This is analogous to finding a marriage partner: it would be unrealistic to expect to find a person who agrees about how the marriage should be lived at every moment. Most of us expect to make small changes in our lives to accommodate the greater good of a fine marriage, but we do not abandon our fundamental beliefs.

Similarly, there are some elements of horn playing, varying from player to player, with which we must be as flexible as possible, and others with which we must be inflexible. Degrees of flexibility vary widely among players concerning such elements as the type of instrument we play, the way we phrase, the tone quality we seek, or the dynamic levels at which we play, as well as what constitutes acceptable conditions of employment. The late horn player Richard Moore used to advise his students to "show a conductor that you are his or her kind of player." I add to his advice only that we must do this from a position of strength and awareness, not out of desperation, weakness, ignorance, or malleability.

In the best possible world, auditioning and everyday music-making would be the same. In the real world, however, they are, in several important ways, different activities, having little to do with each other: auditioning is an outer and public activity performed for an audience; artistic music-making is an inner and personal activity only incidentally shared with an audience. Furthermore, an audition unnaturally emphasizes a single performance, while a concert is most often part of a season of performances.

Some readers will correctly conclude that some of the following suggestions are manipulative. I stress that to perform in an orchestra beautifully we must first be hired— we must jump through a surreal audition "hoop" before we can begin the real task of music-making. This requirement is not unique to music. All fields have their "hoops." Even the late Jonas Salk had to endure some nonsensical aspects of medical school training before he could begin his real work.

In preparing for an audition, it is useful to approximate all circumstances as closely as possible, including both the outer, physical conditions and our inner states. If we are familiar with the acoustical properties of the audition hall, we often can approximate them at home by placing furniture or pillows in strategic places. Occasionally, we can arrange for practice time in the hall itself. Also, we can eat the kind of food we will have before an audition (this is especially useful if we will be traveling to a different region of the country, or to another country entirely), and practice while wearing the clothing we will wear for an audition. It is also helpful to practice on the type of chair we will find in the audition hall. Because of our need to position the bell on the leg, every hornist knows the necessity of adjusting to chairs of varying heights. Of course, this is not a concern

for the increasingly large number of players who hold the
bell free of their leg. Many of us experience out-of-breath, heart-pounding
feelings at an audition. Walking up and down stairs
immediately before starting a mock audition approximates
these feelings and provides opportunities to learn to
compensate for them. For some players, feelings of hunger
also mimic the emotional and physical aspects of
nervousness. (Just as stair-walking and hunger provide
useful opportunities to compensate for the physical
manifestations of nervousness, they also remind us neither
to walk up and down stairs, nor to be hungry, at an
audition.)

Although we often research the business aspects of the
orchestra for which we are auditioning, we sometimes
neglect investigating its musical ones. Do the orchestra and
conductor specialize in a particular repertoire? Does the
conductor have a preference for a specific horn tone? Does
the horn section prefer a specific make of instrument, and if
so, is it flexible about this? Has the orchestra recently
performed compositions featuring a prominent horn solo? If
so, this solo might still be on the conductor's mind. If we
know members of the orchestra, questioning them often
yields such information.

We nearly always are provided with a list of excerpts to
prepare. It is helpful to listen to the orchestra's or the
conductor's recorded version of these compositions, if such
recordings exist. If not, we must practice the excerpts in
many styles, and at various tempi. Also, we should keep
changing the order in which we practice the excerpts. When
we repeatedly "go through the list," we begin to hear the
excerpts as a single "composition." It can be disquieting to

be asked to play the "composition" out of its expected sequence.

For several reasons, it is best to learn the excerpts, or, optimally, the complete horn part from which they are extracted, from actual orchestral parts rather than from excerpt books or even from books containing the complete horn parts. At most auditions we play from actual parts, and visual familiarity with the excerpts—possible only by studying actual parts—affords us a (sometimes crucial) degree of comfort. Furthermore, sometimes the conductor will ask us to continue beyond the portion quoted in the excerpt book, or will ask us to play from a section of the piece he or she suddenly remembers as problematic—even though it is not on the list. We can avoid all of these surprises by learning the excerpts, and the music surrounding them, from orchestral parts.

It is helpful to memorize the excerpts—including, of course, every aspect of the notation. This ensures that the excerpts are given a great deal of attention, and it may provide an informal opportunity to demonstrate knowledge of the repertoire, and, by implication, vast experience performing it.

We must beware of the unwelcome possibility of learning the excerpts incorrectly from an excerpt book; some of the books are carelessly edited. For example, my generation incorrectly learned a solo in the Overture to Gioachino Rossini's *The Barber of Seville* from a then-popular excerpt book.

We also should plan our strategy concerning missteps well in advance. After committing errors we can either request another opportunity to play the passage, or proceed to something new. Correcting the error on the second attempt is helpful, but making the same or a new error is not. The first communicates self-confidence, self-awareness, and good judgment. The latter conveys unrealistic self-confidence, and a lack of both self-awareness and of good judgment.

Whenever feasible, it is best to arrive at the audition site the day before an audition; at the latest, one should arrive four or five hours before the scheduled time. Considering the importance of the occasion, and the energy and money already invested in the event, it is sensible to secure every possible advantage to help us to play at our highest level. Reserving a comfortable hotel room and taking good meals is also part of this strategy. In many ways, an audition trip can be considered to be a short tour, about which more is said in Chapter Three.

Most auditions begin with our playing a composition of our own choosing. Moore's advice on this subject is to "play something that you can play in your sleep." First impressions, whether or not accurate, are strong and often linger. Some conductors will disqualify players immediately after hearing a poorly rendered first offering. Others will politely listen for a few more minutes, but with diminished interest in the player. Most assuredly, we will play "nail-biters" later in the audition, but first must ensure that we will still be there to play them!

We should handle our "warming up" procedure carefully, bearing in mind the physical and emotional disadvantages of warming up insufficiently, too much, or too frequently. If the auditions advance according to the announced schedule, we can base the timing of our usual warm-up patterns on it. If the auditions get ahead of schedule, we must adjust—but "fiercely." If we are not prepared to play due to a change in the audition schedule, we must firmly request sufficient additional time before playing. We must not allow ourselves to be rushed—it is senseless to prepare carefully for an audition, then allow ourselves to be upset by a last-minute change in schedule.

Several strategies are helpful at the final, sight-reading part of an audition. One strategy is to stall for a small amount of time to study the music—by emptying the horn, or by adjusting a slide, the chair, or the music stand. Also, if the audition committee situation allows it, marking the music to remind ourselves of "traps," such as sudden changes of transposition or dynamics, or troublesome rhythms, can prevent missteps. Of course, if the part belongs to the organization for which we are auditioning, we should carefully follow their penciled-in changes. When we are allowed to do it, marking a part helps our playing and, like playing from memory, demonstrates professionalism. The most important aid to the sight-reading component of the audition, however, is accomplished in the years before the audition: learning the repertoire so thoroughly that little will actually *be* sight-read.

Of course, after passing an audition we must work with our new employer. We should accept only a position within which we can live fairly contentedly—while preparing for the next audition. There is also a practical consideration, voiced by Green Bay Packers coach Vince Lombardi: "If you aren't fired with enthusiasm, you will be fired with enthusiasm."

Finally, we should keep a written record of all auditions we take. This helps us to discover our patterns and to preclude repeating mistakes; sometimes small stones can trip us. It is best to make our notations immediately after each audition. They ought to contain everything we remember, including items such as how we learned of the opening, how we prepared musically, what we ate prior to the audition, and how we dressed for it. We should consider both inner and outer aspects for the entire chronology of the event. What did we do? What did the world do?

Bringing newly-achieved fearlessness to an audition, we have already realized considerable inner success, whether or not the results are those for which we had hoped. When we bring long-standing fearlessness, we often also enjoy outer success: we "get the job."

In the healing equation, therefore, the physician brings the best that medical science has to offer, and the patient brings the best that millions of years of evolution have to offer.

                                        —Norman Cousins

III

HEALTH

THE PRECEDING CHAPTERS have addressed mostly the intangible aspects of horn playing such as artistry, awareness, control, and fearlessness. Here, we will consider a tangible aspect: health. Health is important both to ourselves as individuals and, as we shall see in Chapter Four, to the relationships of which we become part. The present chapter draws upon my experience as a hornist, my long-standing interests in medicine and philosophy, gleanings from various types of healers, and personal conclusions. I hope that this material will help readers to reach personal understandings in this vital area. Medical suggestions, coming as they will from a hornist and not a physician, should be considered as only points of departure.

Both scientific and nonscientific truths are represented in this chapter. Rigorously applied, the "scientific method"—identifying a problem, gathering data, forming and testing a hypothesis, and subsequent reproduction of the results by other researchers—uncovers truths. Likewise, the "nonscientific method,"—healing through faith, instinct, and intuition—although lacking in formality, also uncovers truths. Nonscientific truths are not always reproducible, because often they depend on the components of their unique "gestalts," such as unusual physical surroundings, time frames, and variable human sensitivities and awarenesses. This irreproducibility, however, does not lessen the validity of nonscientific truths: recall Gould's statement quoted in the first chapter, "Truth is a circumstance, not a spot." Scientific truth, such as the efficacy of Western synthetic and Eastern natural anti-biotics, are demonstrable and reproducible. Nonscientific truth, such as the Burmese healer's cure described later in this chapter, is based on faith, instinct, and intuition. Knowledge of both scientific and nonscientific truths helps us to view the world synoptically (that is, taking a general view), and enables us to include opposing concepts—such as the thoughts of Darwinists and Creationists, Republicans and Democrats, and the conditions of hot and cold, up and down, alive and dead—in our own viewpoints. We see both Darwinists' physical truths and Creationists' spiritual truths as parts of a larger picture of the Earth's origin; Repub-licans' and Democrats' ideas as parts of the large spectrum of "human political thought;" hot and cold as parts of the larger human concept of "temperature;" "up" and "down" simply as parts of the human concept of "direction;" and "alive" and "dead" as parts of the human concepts of "time" and, possibly, "eternity."

Inclusion, crucial to a synoptic view of the world, is different from compromise, as can be illustrated by imagining two circles. If the circles overlap, the area of overlapping illustrates "compromise." If the circles do not overlap, and a third circle is drawn that encompasses the other two, the large circle illustrates "inclusion." Whether we are dealing with circles, ideas, or people, this principle is the same.

Not surprisingly, many health-related questions may have no answer, one answer, or several answers, because physicians often disagree among themselves. For example, some believe that the herpes simplex type 1 infection (oral herpes) causes cold sores, whereas others consider herpes and cold sores to be different entities. Some doctors consider canker sores to be an auto-immune disease, whereas others consider it to be an infection. Some doctors prescribe only the application of coldness to muscle strains, whereas others order alternating heat and coldness. By retaining our knowledge and instincts regarding medical matters, and simultaneously blending them with those of our physicians, we can form the beneficial relationship (discussed in Chapter Four) that we will call "composite."

My friend Mildred Morganstern, wrote, "I taught my mind to leap. I taught my heart to leap. But alas, my feet...." Her lines acknowledge the physicality that pervades all of life, whether or not we are aware of it. As implied in the concept of *Qi,* even the act of thinking has physical aspects: synapses must fire, chemicals must flow. We are reminded of this physicality when we attempt to think, or to make a genuine choice, while suffering from a headache.

As good health is germane to horn playing, so is our approach to health management. No matter how imaginative our musical ideas, to communicate them we ordinarily need a healthy abdomen, back, lips, teeth, fingers, and arms. As we discussed in Chapter One, however, musicality can sometimes compensate somewhat for physical—and the resultant technical—shortcomings.

Distinctions between general health and horn-playing health are not always easily made; nobody likes a canker sore or the flu. But hornists would be particularly badly affected by certain diseases such as gingivitis and pleurisy, and by conditions such as backaches and hernias. Problems specifically relevant to hornists, therefore, will be addressed separately. We will first, however, examine health and healthcare, allopathy and homeopathy, and general principles of preventive and curative medicine.

HEALTH AND HEALTHCARE

MOST OF US depend upon one or more appropriate "Health Systems" and their particular "Health Practitioners" (Health S/Ps) to help us to prevent and cure health problems. Because few of us innately possess the wisdom of Western allopathic or homeopathic, Indian ayurvedic, Chinese herbal, or Navajo traditional systems and physicians, we must seek out and avail ourselves of their skills. Recently, recognition of the special needs of musicians has resulted in physicians specializing in musician-related problems. These specialists offer varied approaches to these problems, ranging from traditional Western medicine to lesser-known Eastern ones.

Choosing from among the available systems and practitioners is a complicated task. As we have discussed in previous chapters, genuine choices must be based on traits such as application, awareness, fearlessness, and good health. Thus, we must first be aware of alternative possibilities in medicine. Like religions, some S/Ps encourage fearlessness, knowledge, independence, and increased awareness, whereas others foster fearfulness, ignorance, dependence, and unawareness. Choosing our

S/Ps requires finding, within the constraints of time, energy, and financial resources, those that are consistent with our personalities and our values.

Our choices should be based upon our expectations, knowledge, and circumstances. Expectations of good health propel us to seek it; knowledge of health and medicine guides us to appropriate medical intervention (or non-intervention); circumstances provide the practical parameters within which our S/Ps may be chosen.

Further complicating our choices are the myriad definitions of optimum health provided by the myriad S/Ps. In *Disease-Mongers: How Doctors, Drug Companies, and Insurers are Making You Sick* (1992), Lynn Payer states that disease is a human construct, not a definite entity, and that definitions of diseases vary among individuals and from culture to culture. For example, some people consider themselves sick when they have a cold, while others consider colds to be part of everyday life; some consider themselves ill when they are depressed, but others consider normal living to be inherently and unavoidably depressing.

Having clarified various standards of health, we can choose to (1) strive for optimum health, and, if we are able, to feed its correspondingly large appetite for resources; (2) strive for adequate health, with its correspondingly moderate demand for resources; or (3) ignore health issues, freeing ourselves of all burdens associated with healthcare, but possibly in turn becoming burdened with poor health. In other words, we can choose between quantity of life and quality of life, or we can choose a balance between the two.

Most of us would choose a balance; our problem is to find one appropriate for ourselves. Everything we do has ramifications because of connections: time spent at the doctor's office is time away from practicing; money spent for a preventive immunization is money not available for a new mute. In finding our balance between quantity and quality of life we should constantly ask, "What's worth what? Is it wise to spend my time and money for preventive medicine? Should I miss a day's work so that a minor cold will not worsen and cause me to miss a week's work?" Our resources being limited (including time, energy, money, and recuperative powers), asking "what's worth what?" helps to assure that we use these precious resources as awarely and intelligently as possible.

Allopathy and Homeopathy

HAVING DEFINED our goals for health, and ascertained their costs and our resources, we can choose our S/Ps. Those available can be loosely categorized as allopathic (usually, Western medicine) or homeopathic (usually, Eastern medicine). Allopathy, the younger of the two, uses medical and surgical agents to counteract responses to health problems, and reflects the essence of control, as discussed in the previous chapter. Homeopathic medicine is older, uses agents that mimic or augment the body's reactions to invaders, and reflects "spontaneity." Note that Homeopathy (capital "H") refers to a free-standing system of European medicine; we can visit a Homeopathist. These Homeopathic treatments are based on codified herbal tinctures, whereas homeopathic (with a small "h") treatments are based on general homeo-pathic principles which do not necessarily include herbal remedies.

These loose categorizations reflect the "flavors," rather than the details, of allopathy and homeopathy. In addition, there are significant differences within both approaches. For example, the American system of Western medicine views the heart as the central organ, whereas French medicine sees the liver as primary.

As we saw in satire and parody, neither allopathy nor homeopathy exists in a pure form; each always contains elements of the other. Alone, neither system encompasses all human medical knowledge. Each reflects different "voices," or aspects of humanness—different hemispheres of the brain: homeopathy the right, that deals with irrational explanations of the internal world through imagination, instinct and intuition; allopathy the left, that addresses rational explanations of the external world. Together, these systems contain all of the physical and spiritual elements of medicine—the observational, instinctive, and naturally-occurring elements of Eastern-style homeopathic medicine, and the synthesized, intellectual, and man-made elements of Western-style allopathy.

A by-product of the Reformation and Industrial Revolution, allopathy views people as outside nature. Allopathic treatments are often based upon the results of experiments that follow the scientific method, performed in isolation from the world at large. The basic premise of allopathy is that the reactions of a diseased or injured body also are diseased. For example, allopathic medicine prescribes cold-producing agents to counteract the warmth in the area of a muscle sprain. An allopathic plaster cast is applied to a broken limb because, while the limb would heal if left to its own devices, it might heal crookedly.

Allopathy works quickly, often producing dramatic cures. It tends toward specialization that, although effective, can lead to physicians treating their patients as only an isolated gall bladder, knee, or an anonymous accident victim. Allopathic medicine tends toward intervention rather than toward prevention, but often prolongs the quantity of life: our best chance of surviving an automobile accident is to be found in a Western metropolitan hospital.

Homeopathic medicine believes that the body—even a diseased body—possesses innate wisdom that should be heeded. A homeopathic treatment, for example, would use a heat-producing agent on an area already warm in reaction to an injury or an infection. Homeopathic medicine is at ease with the knowledge that not every problem can be cured. It is also comfortable with the pain and death that Western allopathic medicine considers to be its "failures."

Homeopathic medicine addresses quality of life, and in so doing, often prolongs the quantity of life. It very effectively treats chronic conditions such as poor circulation and fatigue. Homeopathic medicine tends toward prevention rather than intervention, and works more slowly than allopathic, often incorporating elements such as spirituality and meditation into its treatments. Homeopathic Hindu, Native American, Chinese, Burmese, Tibetan, and Japanese physicians treat their patients' complete organism—body, mind, and emotions—viewing them in the context of the natural world. A consultation with a traditional homeopathic physician can take several hours.

The lines between allopathy and homeopathy are not irrevocably drawn: homeopathic medicine sometimes uses natural substances in an allopathic manner. For instance, Chinese tea mixtures are often prescribed allopathically to counteract sluggish *Qi*. Likewise, allopathic physicians sometimes borrow homeopathic treatments such as acupuncture. They also acknowledge mind and body connections—usually the domain of homeopathic medicine—through concepts such as "psychosomatic illness" and "the placebo effect." Immunization, one of allopathy's crown jewels, reveals its homeopathic origins in that it activates our natural immune systems. Many allopathic drugs use or mimic naturally occurring plant alkaloids, which are usually the domain of homeopathic medicine. The anti-malarial drug quinine, for example, is derived from the bark of the cinchona tree.

The two views of the world represented by allopathy and homeopathy are not limited to medicine. For instance, when musicians suffer from the "no-desire-to-practice" disease, they sometimes "cure" it by ignoring the problem and practicing nevertheless. On the other hand, they sometimes cure the "disease" homeopathically by obeying their body's innate wisdom and omitting the day's practice. Let us note that this example, while useful to our understanding of allopathy and homeopathy, oversimplifies the "no-desire-to-practice" disease by ignoring the fact that we are not single, unified creatures wanting only to be lazy, or who simply are tired. We contain many inner voices, each clamoring for attention, like a roomful of kindergartners. Thus, until we become more unified, our decision on whether or not to practice will be based on which "voices" shout the loudest.

In the area of health, our loudest inner voices often and unequivocally demand one or the other approach. After bumping our mouths, for example, most of us instinctively (and allopathically) apply coldness to offset the heat and reduce the swelling produced by the increased flow of blood to the area. After a few days, however, the "voices" begin to argue: should we continue to apply allopathic coldness, or should we now apply homeopathic warmth to bring healing blood back to the area? This case illustrates how knowledge of allopathy and homeopathy can guide us to our individually correct course of action. Depending upon the person and circumstances, either course might be correct.

This example also demonstrates how knowledge of several systems of medicine lets us benefit from an array of offerings, rather than being restricted to those of our culture alone. This approach is taken by the famed Texas oncologist O. Carl Simonton, who combines traditional allopathic cancer treatments with Eastern visualization techniques.

Finally, in choosing our S/Ps we also should consider Eastern and Western views of mind and body connections. Generally, Westerners see separations between the mind and the body, whereas Easterners see connections: Westerners see colors and bricks, Easterners see rainbows and walls. Our feelings toward homeopathy and allopathy reflect our answers to certain fundamental questions: Is nature benevolent? Are we a part of nature? If we are a part of nature, are all of our actions *per se* "natural"? What is nature's role in the healing process? Which is more important, our bodies or our society? Am I patient or impatient in a crisis? What are the true sources of health problems?

Having already used the words "nature" and "natural" several times, let us conclude this section with a short examination of this legitimate yet misused word. "Natural" has been so brutalized that a reader of an early version of this chapter, Northern Illinois University Professor of

Philosophy Harold I. Brown, commented that "it is no longer possible to communicate any serious idea with the word 'natural'." Although this point is well taken, I find "natural" to be an important concept when it is carefully defined.

"Natural" thoughts and behaviors are only those that flow without impediment from the chain of energy initiated by the Big Bang. Therefore, "Nature" is the appropriate screen through which to filter everything we think and do. There is, at any given moment, only one completely natural course, although there usually are several other acceptable ones. Natural thoughts and behaviors *belong* in the universe.

The argument is sometimes presented that all that happens is, by definition, "natural" and acceptable. For instance, a "natural" creature, man, invented the atomic bomb; therefore the atomic bomb is a product of nature and, therefore, acceptable. Although this thesis is intellectually defensible, "living" it removes our impetus to better ourselves (by not building bombs) or our world (by eschewing bombs). This type of argument, however, as in the discussion of the "no-desire-to-practice" disease, ignores the many inner voices that comprise the human individual and societal totality. To say that atomic bombs are "natural" is, therefore, only a partial truth. Furthermore, the argument ignores the principle of cause and effect that underlies both individual growth and social change. Finally, and perhaps most importantly, the argument simply ignores common sense.

In the animal world, only humans (and their domesticated animals) exhibit both natural and unnatural behaviors. It is spiritually exhilarating to be in step with the natural world, and natural results *most often* coincide with our desires. The two do not *always* coincide, however. The English philosopher Thomas Hobbes (1588–1679), in *Leviathan,* described man's life as a purely natural creature as "solitary, poor, nasty, brutish, and short."

Neither allopathy nor homeopathy are "natural" systems of medicine. The difference between the two is simply their relative degrees of unnaturalness. Both systems introduce external agents into the body. No matter how natural their source, these agents are not natural to our bodies—at least, not at the time or in the dosages they are administered.

Truly "natural" healing, such as that practiced by The Church of Christ, Scientist, is based on pure spirituality in concert with natural defenses. Christian Science teaches that illness is a product of spiritual "error," and that healing can be effected through prayer, meditation, and by confronting personal issues. Christian Science healings are documented in *Spiritual Healing in a Scientific Age,* by Robert Peel.

Most Western healing arts are allopathic and derive their powers from resources found outside the patient's body, such as chemicals and appliances. Some non-mainstream Western health systems, such as Chiropractic, try simply to remove obstacles (for example, blocked movement of fluids and electrical impulses) to the otherwise inherently wise functioning of the body. In this sense, Chiropractic is homeopathic. Denver Chiropractor Elva Edwards describes her art this way:

> The art and science of Chiropractic is based on the hands-on approach of manipulating the joints of the spine and extremities for the purposes of aligning the bones at the joints, and aborting aberrant neuronal

reflexes that effect the somatic system as well as the
viscera. The intent is to balance the structure (muscles
and bones) of the body in much the same way that an
engineer balances the structure of a building so it is safe
from collapse. Many chiropractors use resources such as
nutrition, acupuncture, herbal and homeopathic preparations, emotional healing, lifestyle choices, and
massage to encourage the patients toward health.
Chiropractors by law cannot prescribe drugs and many
chiropractors consider this an advantage, as it forces us
to get to the root of the problem instead of concealing
the problem through drugs.

Chiropractic medicine has its truths. Mainstream Western
medicine has its truths. As we shall see, homeopathic
Burmese medicine also has its truths. As we become aware
of and encompass seemingly opposite truths—such as those
reflected in allopathic and homeopathic medicine—we gain
insight into the various human inner voices and the nature
of the human brain, and we see the value of inclusion,
rather than exclusion, as we try to understand ourselves and
our world.

Preventive and Curative Medicine

I N *The Lovers,* Ovid rhetorically asks "Isn't the best
defense always a good attack?" In medicine, physicians
unrhetorically answer, "Yes." One aspect of the "good
attack" on health problems is preventive medicine,
including tangible activities such as having routine medical
checkups, and intangible ones such as living spiritually
healthful lives.

For us to practice both preventive and curative medicine
effectively, we must be aware of as many of the available

resources as possible. We also must be aware of principles of preventive and curative medicine, including the nature of cures; the effects of fear, truth, and falsity; the nature of stress; tenets of nutrition; principles of oral health; and the effects of warmth and coldness.

The lines between preventive and curative medicine are not always clearly drawn: many "preventive" measures, such as maintaining healthful sleep patterns, are also curative, and many "curative" measures, such as taking large doses of the vitamin B complex or vitamin C, are also preventive. Most of us are familiar with Western preventive measures, and less familiar with the world's other S/Ps. Traditional Chinese potions exemplify Eastern preventive medicine. They are prepared individually, using the traditional Chinese formulary (composed of more than two thousand plant, animal, and mineral substances), and are prescribed after examining the tongue and eyes, and taking the many pulses. This latter activity is Eastern medicine's most important diagnostic tool, and mastering this subtle and elegant art takes many years. The physician usually measures twelve varying positions and degrees of depth along the radial artery in each wrist, at each position determining the volume, frequency, strength, and rhythm of the pulse. These twelve positions correspond to the twelve "organs" of the body as defined by Eastern medicine. (These "organs" include physical entities such as the heart, but certain energy fields are also considered to be "organs.") There also are up to twenty-eight "qualities" that may be determined, bearing descriptions such as "floating," "thin," "wiry," and "choppy." The pulses indicate the states of the organs and blood, and reveal whether health problems are new or chronic, relatively benign or acute.

Generally, the best cures for health problems are simple, non-invasive, and introduce the smallest amount of foreign material into the body. Side effects are inherent with all drugs, whether they are entirely synthetic or derived from natural substances: no drug produces only one effect. Of course, pressures of time and other considerations sometimes impel us to take a drug. For example, when we are in pain but must perform, most of us gratefully take an allopathic analgesic drug, despite its foreignness to our bodies. Still, we should try to ascertain the cause of the pain, and prevent its future recurrence.

Elevating or lowering injured areas of the body may simply and non-invasively treat problems such as insect bites, swelling, injured or tired muscles, or muscle fatigue. At the end of a tiring day, for example, many of us "put our feet up." Elevating a part of the body decreases the amount of blood, and consequently the warmth, of that region, whereas lowering it increases the flow of blood. How to determine when and whether to lower or to elevate an injured area is not always clear. When we are unsure of which way, if any, to "lean" (so to speak), allopathic and homeopathic principles, as well as our intuitions, often provide guidance.

Building and maintaining muscle strength and agility, either through exercise or such systems as Alexander Technique and Feldenkreis, may prevent or cure health problems such as soreness, strains, sprains, and hernias. There are many ways, both aerobic and anaerobic, to build and maintain muscle strength, but regimens should be minimally stressful. Otherwise, we simply substitute one problem (stress) for another (weak musculature).

Maintaining correct sitting, standing, walking, and sleeping postures simply and non-invasively helps us to prevent or treat muscle soreness and stiffness, as well as injury to internal organs. Correct posture, emphasized in Chiropractic medicine and Alexander Technique, also enables us to breathe deeply, thereby helping to prevent respiratory problems. Deep breathing, in turn, promotes the circulation of blood and lymphatic fluids.

Finally, following sensible sleep, rest, and vacation patterns simply and non-invasively helps us to prevent or cure various health problems by allowing time for the body, mind, and spirit to heal and rejuvenate. Many problems heal more quickly when we "sleep them off." Some, such as mononucleosis, effect their own (homeopathic) cure by increasing our fatigue. This is especially important, even miraculous, in the case of mononucleosis, since sleep and rest are the only Western treatments for the disease. Too much sleep, however, can weaken our immune systems, as well as cause swelling. We should try to include enough sleep in our daily lives so that we may recuperate, but not so much that we become weak or lethargic.

Whether they are invasive or non-invasive, we must be circumspect about "cures": under- or overused cures can themselves cause illness. For instance, if antibiotics are underprescribed or taken for too short a time, the stage can be set for superinfection. Conversely, vitamins A and D can be deadly if taken in excess. Furthermore, problems can arise if we become habituated to—and dependent on—what is intended to be only a "temporary" cure, such as a brace for the back or wrist, or narcotic-based cough medicines.

Complicating our understanding of "cures" is the human ability to adjust to circumstances. This ability is a double-edged sword. Its positive side is seen in our ability to adjust appropriately to adversities such as asthma or a rude colleague. Its negative side is our ability to adjust to adversities that more sensibly could be changed or eliminated. An example of misused resilience (achieved through misusing will power) to overcome "fears which it would be more advantageous to eliminate altogether" in order to play the "long call" from *Siegfried*, was cited in the previous chapter. Another example of this misuse would be our learning to tolerate a painful but curable condition, rather than seeking a cure for the condition. Awareness of this double-edged sword helps us to distinguish the difference between enjoying good health and accommodating poor health. Along these lines, it is important to be aware of our individual, normal rates of healing: if we know what is normal for our bodies, we consequently know what is *ab*normal. This knowledge can help us to determine if a condition is persisting, and, therefore, of a possibly serious nature.

Routine preventive medical tests, such as those that determine lipid profiles and blood sugars, test vision, and measure blood pressure, establish "baselines." These should then be compared to future test results so that we may discern trends that can alert us to problems in their early stages. For instance, even a slight change in blood sugar levels can warn us of the possible onset of diabetes.

We should be aware that physical "places of change" (i.e., beginnings, endings, and junctions) are especially prone to problems. These areas of change can be of an active (we are doing something) or passive (our *bodies* are making the change, without our input) nature. For example, when we begin to move our hands, we actively produce places of change at our wrists and fingers, and perhaps also our arms and shoulders. On the other hand, the change in the blood supply between the skin of the face and lips, made evident by the difference in skin color and the tendency of lip tissue to bleed more readily, is a passive change. In the interest of preventive medicine, we should give extra attention to places of change; in diagnosing problems, places of change should be our first "suspects."

Places of change also occur, of course, outside the body. In music-making, for example, these include the beginnings and ends of notes (where sound is joined with silence or with other notes), and junctions of sections within a composition, such as between a minuet and trio. Nonmusical places of change include taking off in an airplane (joining earthbound with airborne), and merging into automobile traffic (joining slowly moving traffic with faster traffic).

Fear's negative impacts on our health are well known: for example, fear raises our stress levels, blood pressure, and heart rates. Fearlessness helps to prevent mental problems—for example, paranoia ("the conductor is out to get me")—by removing the erroneous view of fear as a viable stance. In addition, fearlessness helps to alleviate physical problems such as excess body tension.

Perhaps most importantly, as mentioned in Chapter Two, fearlessness is a facet of truth, which can, in turn, produce beneficial health effects. The fearless embracing of truth can sometimes cure even seemingly incurable problems. An example of such a cure, similar in "flavor" to Christian Science healing, was related by Rina Sircar, a Burmese Buddhist nun and healer, at a conference held at the Naropa Institute, in Boulder, Colorado, in June, 1986.

She described treating a boy who had received an ordinarily lethal snake bite. Her treatment consisted of asking the townspeople to encircle the boy and to reveal previously unconfessed truths about themselves. This was asking a lot of the community—that they make their revelations fearless of embarrassment, reprisal, scorn, or rejection. By clearing the area of untruths, such as lies told and artificial walls built between community members, the "circle of truth" enabled the boy to concentrate on his rather grave truth (the snake bite) without outside distraction. Having a young, otherwise healthy body, the boy was then able to recover.

On the other hand, un-truth, whether arising from ignorance or malice, can produce deleterious health effects by preventing us from benefitting from others' truths, including those regarding health. George Bernard Shaw (1856–1950) wrote that "the liar's punishment is not in the least that he is not believed, but that he cannot believe anyone else."

It also is helpful, as both a preventive and curative measure, to limit our mental and physical stresses to necessary and manageable levels. Excessive mental stress can contribute to stroke or heart attack. Excessive, or even merely constant, physical stress, such as is caused by a foreign substance—a metal mouthpiece, for example—on lip tissue, can predispose us to tumors. While not entirely unavoidable, both physical and mental strains can be minimized by applying them to only the task at hand, for the minimum possible amount of time, and only to the degree necessary to accomplish the task. For example, the physical stress on the lips caused by the mouthpiece can be minimized by practicing efficiently, and by removing the mouthpiece from the lips whenever feasible. Mental stress can be limited by focusing only on the real problems of music-making. In addition, we can reduce the stress levels in our everyday lives by limiting our activities and possessions, learning Eastern homeopathic breathing and meditation techniques, and by following prudent work, sleep, dietary, exercise, and vacation patterns.

Nutrition, too, can both prevent and treat health problems: diet is frequently sufficient to cure a condition, or can be used as an adjunct to other treatments. What, when, and how much to eat are obviously important choices. They also are personal choices: some of us eat meat, some do not; some of us eat before playing, others do not; some of us eat a lot, some eat little.

Knowledge of diverse viewpoints should underlie our dietary decisions. These viewpoints range from the traditional Western food group distinctions, to those of the Indian Ayurvedic diet based on "doshas" (individual body- and mind classifications determined by reading the patient's several pulses, observing their body types, and ascertaining their personality traits through interviews), to the Japanese macrobiotic diet (based on cooked, locally grown produce, designed to balance bodily sodium and potassium—our physical yin and yang). Ayurvedic and macrobiotic diets exemplify eating patterns incorporated into spiritual or philosophical systems.

Diet and supplements can, of course, be altered to adjust our intake of nutrients such as vitamins, digestion-aiding fiber, minerals, and protein. The use of supplements is controversial. Some people believe that nutrients in supplement form cannot be adequately absorbed, and that they are, in fact, useless. Some feel that our national food supply is so degraded by chemicals and staleness that it cannot adequately nourish us, and that supplements are useful. Another group believes that we can be adequately nourished by conventional foods; still others believe that we can obtain adequate nutrients only from carefully selected foods obtainable only at specialty shops, and they are willing to pay the high costs, both in energy and money, attendant to doing so. As is true elsewhere, our dietary decisions should be based on our answers to the question, "What's worth what?"

Practically all dietary systems advise either no or restricted use of alcohol and tobacco. In some cultures, however, alcohol and/or hallucinogens are considered so important to the society that their negative physical effects are thought to be outweighed. Most Western and Eastern nutritional systems, however, recommend that we limit our dietary fats, and especially saturated and hydrogenated fats. We should seriously consider this recommendation: while much medical advice changes constantly, this advice has been consistently offered for many years. Also, most Eastern and Western medicines advocate the maintaining of a moderate body weight, both to minimize strain on the heart and skeleton, and—possibly (physicians disagree)—to lower blood pressure and heart rate.

The external application of either warmth or coldness to a part of the body can have positive or negative effects when used either preventively or curatively. Warmth draws blood and its healing antibodies to an area, but this also encourages swelling; coldness reduces blood flow and the attendant swelling in an area, and also isolates and numbs it, but coldness can also slow the rate of healing of some kinds of injuries. Before deciding whether to apply warmth or coldness to an injured area, we should first ascertain whether it really is hot. An injured area often "feels" hot to us merely because of the attention we give it. We should seek a second thermal opinion.

Application of moist or dry warmth or coldness in various combinations are also common treatments. For example, either dry or moist warmth, such as is provided by a dry heating pad or a warm, moist towel, brings blood to an area. Both are commonly prescribed for muscle injuries. Dry warmth concentrates the fluid material of infections, allowing them to be easily drained. Dry warmth is often recommended for small, localized infections, such as small pimples, which we can carefully drain without professional guidance. Large boils, on the other hand, should be treated professionally. Since moisture, whether warm or cold, encourages bacterial growth, we should keep infected areas dry.

For most muscle injuries, both Western and Eastern physicians often first advise dry coldness (for example, ice in a plastic bag), then moist warmth after pain and swelling have subsided. Not surprisingly, homeopathic doctors advise moist warmth on a moist, warm area (for instance, a warm gargle for a sore throat), and dry warmth on a dry, warm injury, such as a strained muscle.

Maintaining the coolest comfortable body temperature is another preventive measure: coolness inhibits both the acquisition and growth of many pathogens. With minimal planning we can keep clothing close at hand for unanticipated indoor or outdoor conditions. A lightweight summer tuxedo, a heavyweight one for winter, or a sweater stored in the trunk of the car for an unexpectedly cool evening band concert, can prevent discomfort and other health problems.

Preventive and Curative Medicine for Hornists

WE NOW APPLY preventive and curative medicine specifically to horn players. Not surprisingly, many hornists' afflictions are found in areas of the body involved in playing, such as the head, neck, abdomen, arms, hands, and lower back. In addition, problems in other parts of the body can cause discomfort that often communicates itself into our tone, affects our endurance, and diverts our attention from playing.

Whether we are sitting or standing with the horn, our posture when playing should be the same as our normal posture. We should adjust the instrument to our usual posture, not the opposite. This sometimes requires bending or resetting the leadpipe, or adjusting the "pinky ring." Some of us find that a small brace placed between the thumb and first finger of the left hand (sometimes called a "duck's foot"), allows the wrist, hand, and fingers to be as comfortable as possible. Air technique includes compression of the air column, requiring the coordinated efforts of many muscles. Good posture disperses these efforts so that no muscle is overly burdened, thus helping to prevent problems such as inguinal and umbilical hernias.

We can take our cue from the trail hikers' practice of incorporating rest into each step they take. For hornists this means pacing ourselves carefully during practice, rehearsal, and performance sessions, and taking the mouthpiece off our lips as often as possible. (This is distinct from the previous suggestion to remove the mouthpiece frequently to minimize irritation to lip tissue.) Pacing ourselves also includes not overbooking our work commitments. This is often easier said than done.

Finally, because they strongly affect the health of the mouth and nervous system, vitamins A, the B complex, and D, are most relevant to horn playing. Also important are vitamins E for cardiovascular health, and C for prevention of infections.

Let us now examine, from head to toe, health problems with special impacts on hornists. Our scope will be limited to less common problems, lesser known treatments for common problems, and those problems to which hornists are especially susceptible.

First of all, headaches commonly afflict hornists. Most of our headaches originate from benign causes such as proximity to the percussion section, or from eyestrain caused by the poor lighting we often find in an orchestra pit. Medical students are taught, "If you hear hoofbeats, first think of horses, not zebras." Headaches may, however, occasionally indicate serious conditions. Recurrent or persistent headaches, even of seemingly identifiable origin, should be precisely diagnosed because of the chance of finding a "zebra."

The obvious solution for headaches caused by loud sounds is to move away from them. If this is not possible, an indirect if uncomfortable solution is to wear cotton earplugs. Headaches due to eyestrain can be prevented by eyeglasses or contact lenses of appropriate strength, either of which must allow us both to see the music, which is rather close to us, as well as the relatively far away conductor. Tinted lenses are useful in pits with especially bright lights on the music stands.

Many of hornists' health problems involve the mouth area. Oral preventive medicine begins with brushing and flossing the teeth, both of which help to prevent cavities, gingivitis, canker sores, and Vincent's disease (also called "Vincent's angina" and "trench mouth"). Other preventive measures include periodic—perhaps the often-advised two times per year—dental and periodontal check-ups, and regular use of lip moisturizers to help prevent chapping and peeling of the lips. For those predisposed to angular cheilosis (sores at the corners of the mouth, formerly called "angular cheilitis"), routine use of moisture barriers, such as heavy ointments, helps to keep saliva away from the corners of the mouth. Bacterial lip infections that are caused by contamination of the pores around them may be prevented by refraining from touching our lips with our (non-sterile) hands.

The uniqueness of our playing, and especially of our tone, depends in part upon the interactions of the angles and surfaces contained within our mouths, and upon the shape of our oral chambers. A tooth that, to our eyes, has moved imperceptibly will quickly make itself known to our ears. For this reason, we ought to maintain a current, professionally made cast of our teeth. These are usually made of plaster or "die stone," which is more durable. If it becomes necessary, due to an accident, disease, or if teeth have shifted, a cast may enable a dentist to restore our teeth—and our horn playing—to their previous condition.

The necessary breathing through the mouth for full as well as "catch" breaths often dries the mouth and throat tissues, thus making us relatively susceptible to respiratory infections. Wetting our throats with saliva at every opportunity, and breathing through the nose during rests can somewhat offset this dryness. When we are "off duty," drinking liquids and using throat-soothing lozenges helps to prevent throat soreness and colds.

Male horn players should allow sufficient time before the next playing session for the inevitable small cuts and irritations associated with shaving around the mouth to heal. This simple approach can prevent them from having to play with irritated or cut lips. Both genders can both prevent and heal chapped lips by using common softening or sunblocking preparations. In addition to these, other effective balms are vitamin A and D ointment, lanolin, Peterson's Ointment, cocoa butter, olive oil, and Mentholatum. Some preparations, such as Elizabeth Arden Eight Hour Cream, can be retained on the lips while playing, and are a boon to hornists living in dry or cold climates.

Sharp-edged or misaligned teeth can irritate our inner cheeks and gums. Any irritation that is not allowed to heal can potentially lead to serious health problems over time. These problems are in addition to the problems specific to playing, such as uneven seating of the mouthpiece that cripples tone quality, flexibility, endurance, range, and control of dynamics. Problem teeth should be filed or even moved, but only by a physician familiar with the subtleties of horn playing, and only after she or he has studied the player's embouchure setting on his or her mouthpiece.

Gingivitis (gum inflammation) is most commonly caused by bacteria that are at the root of the plaque-to-tartar-to-inflammation process. The process can be forestalled by gentle brushing and flossing of our teeth and gums to remove the bacteria. We should beware that too much brushing or flossing can themselves produce irritation-related gingivitis. Most often, the treatment for bacterial gingivitis is direct and allopathic, and includes thoroughly cleaning our teeth and gums, and rinsing with slightly salty warm water, perhaps repeatedly. Gingivitis can also be caused by stress, or hormonal changes such as those associated with pregnancy. If stress is the cause, the treatment is to lower our stress levels. If pregnancy is the cause, the problem is self-limiting.

Canker sores are smooth or slightly raised ulcers in the mouth or on the outer border of the lips. Physicians disagree about their cause: bacteria, stress, endocrine changes, food allergies, and shortages of dietary vitamin B12, folic acid, and iron are implicated. Some physicians believe that canker sores are viral, internal versions of herpes. Other doctors believe that canker sores and herpes are unrelated. Some players suffer recurring canker sores, lending evidence to the virus theory, whereas others contract canker sores only once, lending credence to the bacteria theory. There is no permanent cure for canker sores, although prescribed topical steroids help reduce the swelling and, for some players, tincture of myrrh temporarily relieves the pain of canker sores. In addition, warm salt water rinses help to promote healing.

Oral herpes (also called, confusingly, cold sores or fever blisters) is an opportunistic and tenacious viral infection. Herpes produces painful sores, blisters, rashes, lesions, ulcers, and swelling. These sores most often occur outside the mouth, but sometimes appear on the inside. The virus establishes itself during times of lowered disease resistance caused by trauma, stress, abrasion, sunburn, fever, aging, menstruation, or allergies. Oral herpes, although self-limiting, can lead to secondary bacterial infections.

Herpes infection can be controlled, but not cured. Most often the virus remains in the body, flaring periodically. Fortunately, the time between attacks typically lengthens, and sometimes the disease becomes asymptomatic. Drugs can occasionally alleviate the swelling and pain of oral herpes. Allopathic physicians disagree about the efficacy and safety of drugs such as acyclovir pills and ointment, and of procedures such as irradiating dye-painted herpes sores with ultraviolet light. They also disagree about the efficacy of increasing dietary lactic acid through tablets or through foods such as yogurt. Players who have had success using lactic acid find that it is most effective if taken prior to expected trauma, stress, abrasion, and so on.

"Trench mouth" is an overgrowth of oral bacteria which are normally present. It most commonly afflicts teenagers and young adults opportunistically, thriving amid conditions such as poor oral hygiene, high stress levels, and low immunity. Trench mouth often causes the gums to shrink, bleed, turn grayish, and to produce a strong odor. The most common treatments are Western, and include lowering the patient's stress levels, surgically removing the infected tissue and foreign matter from the area (a procedure called "débridement"), and prescribing mouth-washes of diluted peroxide, warm salt water, or antibiotics.

Angular cheilosis, the development of painful cracks (or, according to one physician, cold sores) at the corners of the mouth, results from a nutritional deficiency (usually, of protein or B vitamins) or from a bacterial, viral, or fungal infection. When the cause is dietary, the treatment is restoration of the missing nutrients. When the cause is bacterial, an effective allopathic treatment is the application of non-drying antibiotic ointments. When the cause is viral, Western medicine cannot offer an effective treatment. When the cause is fungal, allopathy can offer antifungal ointments. Homeopathic (capital "H") herbal antibiotics are sometimes successful at treating the disease, even when it is of viral origin.

The neck and shoulder areas easily accumulate tension that can communicate itself into the horn tone. Simple routines such as occasionally shrugging the shoulders or gently rotating the neck help to prevent the build-up of tension in these areas. Such tensions often can be relieved by various types of homeopathic and allopathic massage (such as Jin Shin Jyutsu, Swedish, and Rolfing), and Yogic postures. Also helpful are chiropractic manipulation, exercises for strengthening the region, homeopathic or allopathic balms, and Chinese and Japanese acupuncture. Acupuncture is especially effective in treating headaches, as well as wrist, elbow, and lower back pain.

The common Western treatments for muscle strain—a muscle taxed or stretched beyond its normal limit—are rest, cold compresses, and elevation of the area. After a few days, most physicians advise using warmth to increase the blood in the area. The treatment for muscle sprain—bruised or twisted muscle fiber—is the same. On the other hand, torn or ruptured muscle tissue is a serious condition, often requiring surgical intervention.

Lower back pain is effectively treated with Eastern and Western massage, Yoga stances, acupuncture, stretching exercises, and improved posture. Chiropractic massage, chemical muscle relaxants, and appliances such as braces and bandages also are effective. We must, however, avoid dependency on any of these, so that they do not become medical counterparts of courage, hiding genuine problems and precluding genuine cures.

Although we hornists use our hands to a lesser extent than most of our orchestra colleagues, we must be sure to use them in manners that prevent injury or discomfort. We can prevent pain in our hands, as well as improve our technique at both ends of the horn, by keeping the fingers of our left hands as relaxed as possible, and the fingers of our right hands both relaxed and parallel to each other, not allowing them to overlap in the bell. Carpal tunnel syndrome is unusual for hornists, but not unheard of. Keeping both wrists relaxed, and gently shaking them periodically, can help to prevent this debilitating condition.

The stuffiness, lethargy, and fever of respiratory infections such as common colds strongly affect horn playing. More seriously, untreated colds can progress to bacterial or viral pleurisy—inflammation of the "pleura," the delicate membrane covering the lungs and lining the chest cavity—producing intense chest pain and painful breathing. The Western treatments for bacterial pleurisy are rest and antibiotics. For viral pleurisy, rest and the good offices of our immune systems effect the cure. For either type of pleurisy, deep breathing, although painful, is essential to preventing the development of pneumonia.

We also can practice preventive medicine on the horn itself. Brushing our teeth, or at the least rinsing the mouth before playing, helps to keep the instrument's tubing and valve casings free of food particles and saliva-borne pathogens. Routinely using a flexible cleaning "snake" and flushing the leadpipe and tubing with warm water removes the food particles and pathogens that elude the toothbrush. We also should avoid lubricating valves and slides with toxic oils and greases, since these can be accidentally ingested through the mouthpiece or by transference from our hands.

Wrapping the areas of the instrument that are in contact with the skin helps to prevent allergic reactions to the metal. For those who need them, hypo-allergenic mouthpieces are available, made of plastics, natural substances such as wood, and hypo-allergenic metals such as gold and platinum. These materials prevent both skin and digestive allergies. Finding suitable alternatives to metal mouthpieces often requires much trial and error: mouthpiece materials must provide a balance between smoothness (so that we can easily move our lips), and roughness (so that we can anchor them to the mouthpiece).

TOURING

It is more difficult to maintain good health on tour than it is at home. While traveling, we contend with constantly changing dietary and sleep patterns, altitude, humidity, and temperature. Preventive medicine becomes more important on the road because it must also offset the musical stresses of touring, such as the challenges of adjusting to chairs of different heights and of performing in unfamiliar acoustics.

Before we embark on tour it is wise to prepare extra eyewear and essential medications for quick, emergency shipment should the need arise, and to carry prescriptions for both. This is especially important when traveling in other countries. In addition, simple prevention counsels us to preclude the loss of essentials such as eyeglasses or medication by packing them in carry-on bags only: luggage is occasionally misplaced by airlines.

On tour, normal life patterns of personal hygiene, exercise, medication, and the like should be retained whenever possible. There will, however, be unavoidable differences, since we cannot take our waterbeds or completely adhere to our usual dietary or sleep patterns. Special circumstances, however, can sometimes be accommodated. Players with back problems, for example, can sometimes arrange for a special chair to be transported. Because of the increased need for stamina while touring, we should adhere to our usual exercise routines, or establish new ones. While on the airplane, train, or bus, maintaining good posture and moving, stretching, and shrugging help to prevent muscle stiffness caused by physical inactivity. We should also avoid mental stiffness. Stimulating books, tapes, or movies keep our minds and souls alert amid the sometimes mind- and soul-numbing aspects of life on the road.

Diet is easily disrupted while touring. With effort, we can minimize this disruption by seeking restaurants serving the kind of food we want, by bringing food with us, or by cooking in our hotel rooms. A healthful and nutritious diet, perhaps bolstered by supplements, keeps us healthy, lifts our spirits, and prevents the feeling, common among touring musicians, of "coming down with something." Although to save money we sometimes prudently skimp on hotel or entertainment costs, we ought not to do so at the expense of normal dietary habits. Especially on working days, we should adhere as closely as possible to our normal diets, reserving experiments with unfamiliar cuisines for days off.

Sleep patterns, too, are easily disrupted on tour, especially if we constantly cross time zones. Study of the itinerary prior to the tour can help us to foresee potential sleep-deprivation situations, and we can sleep extra hours in anticipation of them. Homeopathic ear and underarm massage remedies for jet lag are sometimes effective, and can be self-administered.

Changing altitudes, temperatures, and humidities are other factors for which we can prepare. For example, we can prepare for the diminished oxygen supply at high altitude by increasing our dietary iron. We can prepare for temperature variations by bringing clothing adequate for temperature extremes, and we can anticipate extremely dry conditions by bringing an extra-large supply of our favorite moisturizer.

The many challenges of touring require both routine and extra preventives. If we perform them well, and approach with flexibility and good humor the necessary changes to our routines, we can remain healthy and enjoy the excitement and changes of life on the road. Whether we are on tour or at home, allopathic and homeopathic preventives and curatives help to keep us healthy. In turn, our healthy state enables us to add healthy ingredients to healthy relationships—as we will discuss in the following chapter.

As we live, we are transmitters of life.
And when we fail to transmit life, life fails to flow
    through us.

—D. H. Lawrence

IV
RELATIONSHIPS

IN THIS CHAPTER we will examine horn sections in a
new way: as relationships that combine into ever more
complex webs. Understanding these webs helps us to
form vital horn sections, and to improve less-than-vital
ones. At the center of all of these webs are our inner
voices, simultaneously issuing commands such as "Eat that
cake!" and "Don't eat that cake!" or "Observe that slur!"
and "Ignore that slur!" In horn sections, the center then
expands to include relationships among the members of
the section, then to incorporate relationships between the
section and the rest of the brass section, spinning outward
to encompass the orchestra, the audience, and the
macrocosm that is the universe.

Horn sections are not isolated entities. Rather, they are
products of the chain of energy started by the Big Bang
many millions of years ago. This chain stretches into the
past, present, and future, and into all reaches of the
universe. Being part of the chain of energy, everything

about the section affects the macrocosm. The macrocosm in turn affects everything about the section.

Everything in the universe, whether tangible or intangible, exists within contexts such as time, space, temperature, and gravity. Faraway Pluto exerts gravitational and thermal influences upon us just as surely as does our morning cup of coffee. Pondering the Big Bang's effect on our lives raises a question similar to that raised by control, which was addressed in Chapter Two: If we are part of an all-encompassing chain of energy, how much do our actions matter? The answer is similar to that suggested earlier: if we wish to be as effective as possible within the energy chain, yet we do not know for certain how or if our actions affect this chain, to ensure our best efforts we must behave as if our efforts matter.

Relationships, both in everyday living and within horn sections, have implications on our understanding of both microcosms and the macrocosm. Pondering relationships in general and the relationships within horn sections in particular raises many questions: How ought each member of a horn section to relate to him- or herself? How should section members relate to each other? How can a section relate to the rest of the brass section, the orchestra, the conductor, the composer, the audience, the state, the country, the continent, ad infinitum? How can a section distinguish between inevitabilities, possibilities, and impossibilities?

To confront such questions we must first define several terms. "Autonomy," "near autonomy," and "dependency" refer to relationships within ourselves, and they may exist either alone or as parts of larger relationships. "Mixture," "compound," and "composite" are the relationships relevant to our discussion. The terms are borrowed from chemistry, and refer to various combinations of two or more substances. In a mixture, the substances are not chemically bound to each other, whereas in a compound they are bound, resulting in an independent identity unlike any of the original components. "Composite" will be used here to describe relationships in which entities are simultaneously in mixture and compound relationships with each other. The resultant relationship, the composite, is a new product (therefore it is compound-like), but the components do not wholly lose their identities (therefore it is also mixture-like).

UNITS OF RELATIONSHIPS

Autonomy, Near Autonomy, and Dependency

OUR WORLD is comprised of "near autonomies" and "dependents," and there is a continuum between them. "Autonomy" means complete self-sufficiency and, if it existed, would include any completely self-sufficient unit, be it a person, plant, inanimate object, and so on. Complete autonomy, however, does not exist: the Dutch philosopher Benedict de Spinoza (1632–1677) taught that only the "totality"—the macrocosm—is completely self-sufficient. In the same spirit, the English poet John Donne (1573–1631) wrote, "No man is an island." In our daily lives and experiences, complete autonomy is only an ideal, a concept. The term "near autonomy" means a state of approaching autonomy. At the other end of the spectrum, "dependency" means a state of distance from autonomy. While "near autonomy" and "dependency" can refer to relationships either between animate or inanimate entities, in this discussion these terms will apply to humans, unless otherwise stated.

Although complete autonomy is impossible for humans to attain, the concept of autonomy is useful. Like full awareness, complete control, and perfection (this last to be discussed in Chapter Five), the concept of autonomy establishes an unachievable goal for which we ought nevertheless to strive, using all of the application, awareness, fearlessness, belief in the goodness of the universe, and physical well-being at our disposal. Although we cannot become completely autonomous, we can, and should, become nearly autonomous. Even near autonomy, however, must not be an end in itself. Rather, it should be the means through which we achieve the purest possible relationship to everything in the universe; the self-empathy which characterizes autonomy should also be used to increase empathy toward all that which is not ourselves.

Near autonomies derive most of their characteristics from within. They know who they are and they are sure of their correct paths, like great spiritual leaders or Siberian tigers. Nearly autonomous people, possessing large amounts of self-sufficiency and self-direction, can choose the relationships into which they enter.

There is a correlation between our degrees of awareness and our degrees of autonomy. Perhaps the correlation is that autonomy is built on inner awareness, and that one facet of inner awareness is awareness of inner resources. Completely autonomous people would be completely aware; nearly autonomous people are highly aware.

Near autonomies can choose to be in (1) mixtures—retaining their characteristics, and not melding into the other entities; (2) compounds—giving up all or part of their characteristics, and blending into other entities for a perceived ultimate gain; or (3) composites—retaining their individuality and simultaneously incorporating into new entities. Of the three relationships, near autonomies most often choose mixtures or composites.

Dependents are far indeed from autonomy. They are like clouds, constantly changing shape and direction, defined by outer circumstances rather than by inner promptings. They are relatively unaware; they can neither make choices nor be present in the moment. Not being fully developed emotionally or spiritually, dependents exhibit fearfulness and a paucity of focus, awareness, and artistry. In addition, they tend to be mired in the past, present, or future rather than to be at ease with the time-continuum.

As a result of these traits, dependents are limited to being drawn into compounds with people, and to "identification" with inanimate objects or experiences. "Identification" produces a condition wherein dependent people automatically relinquish themselves, and thereby are engulfed by inanimate objects or experiences. "Identification" is a *behavior* rather than a relationship, although "identification" has similarities to mixtures and compounds. For instance, both "identification" and compounds produce mergers, although "identification" completely overwhelms at least one of the components, whereas the inanimate objects or experiences are not perceptibly changed. In Chapter Five we will return to "identification" in our discussion of nearly-autonomous specific perfectionism.

RELATIONSHIPS

Mixtures, Compounds, and Composites

MIXTURES are composed of near autonomies that retain their individual characteristics. Elements of mixtures neither bond with each other nor do they produce a new relationship that is itself a new entity. To human perceptions, these near autonomies do not affect each other, but simply coexist within a defined area.

Mixtures are common relationships. For instance, oil-and-vinegar salad dressing is a mixture. Both ingredients retain their characteristics, do not bond with the other, and have no perceivable influences on each other. Oil and vinegar, however, like components of any mixture, do have humanly imperceptible gravitational and thermal effects on each other. Mixtures cannot be formed solely by dependents (only compounds can do this, as we shall see), but mixtures can be formed by a dependent entity and an inanimate object. For example, a mixture is formed by a dependent person holding an inanimate pencil.

Compounds are composed of dependent entities that lose, or (less commonly) near autonomies that voluntarily relinquish, all or most of their characteristics, bond with each other, and form a relationship that is itself a new entity. The components of compounds have humanly perceptible influences on each other.

Like mixtures, compounds are common relationships. For example, water, comprised of hydrogen and oxygen gasses, is a compound. In becoming water, the hydrogen loses its individuality as an explosive gas, the oxygen loses its individuality as a supporter of fire, and their new relationship forms a non-explosive entity that can extinguish fire. Another compound, Russian dressing, contains mainly tomato paste and mayonnaise. These two elements can form a new entity (Russian dressing) in which both give up many of their individual characteristics and bond with each other.

There is an easily observed difference between the earlier oil-and-vinegar mixture and the present Russian dressing compound. This difference helps us to distinguish between the two types of relationships. If the two dressings are left standing, we see the unbonded oil and vinegar mixture separate into its components, whereas the bonded Russian dressing compound does not.

True composites are simultaneously mixtures and compounds. Miraculously, they keep the attributes of both. They alone retain individualities while simultaneously establishing new entities. Because humans cannot be fully autonomous we cannot achieve true composite relationships. Lewis Thomas' description of an anthill, summarized in Chapter One, as both a collection of ants ("antities"?) and, simultaneously, an independent organism, describes a near composite: the individual ants are nearly autonomous, the ant hill organism is nearly autonomous, and the relationship between the two is a near composite. Wild insects, like wild plants and animals (and unlike humans) are nearly autonomous and form near composites with their environments, provided that these are also wild. On the other hand, domesticated insects such as farm bees, domesticated plants such as hybridized corn, and domesticated animals like the family dog, are dependent compared to their wild counterparts. Having lost some their "bee-ness," "corn-ness," or "dog-ness," they can form only compounds with animate beings, or mixtures with inanimate objects.

Near composites are by far the most valuable relationships, and by far the most difficult to attain, since they demand application, awareness, fearlessness, and continual growth. The transcendent difficulty of achieving near "composite-ness" is its requirement that we be in two places at once: "here" and "there." Although being in two places at once is illogical by ordinary standards, a highly aware near autonomy in a near composite relationship can indeed be here and there—if not corporeally, then mentally and spiritually. A ride in an airplane illustrates "here" and "there." From the ground, we see only a small amount of territory, corresponding in "flavor" to the "here" of unawareness and dependency. On the other hand, from the air we see much more, including what we see from the ground. This corresponds in "flavor" to the "here" of unawareness and the "there" of awareness and near autonomy. In other words, if we are unaware and dependent, our view of ourselves and of the universe is small. As we become more aware and more nearly autonomous our view becomes commensurately larger.

Near composites can contain only near autonomies, either animate or inanimate. Familiar near composites formed by animate and inanimate objects are those containing ourselves (if we are nearly autonomous) and our instruments: our animate, nearly autonomous selves remain ourselves, our inanimate nearly autonomous horns remains themselves, and, simultaneously, we form distinct horn playing entities. Marriages are other possible near composites. Marriages in which husbands live independent lives, wives live independent lives, and the couples (the marriage entities) live yet other independent lives, are near composites. With apologies to Humphrey Bogart, near composites are the best starts of beautiful friendships. Music-making depends on near composites. Two examples are counterpoint, in which each voice exists independently while simultaneously contributing to a larger, independent musical entity, and the effective communication of a musical line that demands that our senses of past, present, and future form a composite within ourselves. This composite enables us to distinguish between, yet simultaneously integrate, past, present, and future parts of the composition. Artistic music-making requires that each note communicate where it came from, why it presently exists, and where it will go.

An ideal world would consist of a hierarchy of composites (each, by definition, composed of autonomies), producing composites upon composites upon composites. Such a world would refute Spinoza's teaching that only the macrocosm is self-sufficient. Our world and our species being less than ideal, however, the most we human beings can add to it is our near autonomy. Spinoza remains unrefuted.

Near composites reflect the "healthy chauvinism" of, for example, a healthy nation. While ordinary chauvinism is the unaware and fear-based pride that one's nation is superior to others, healthy chauvinism, based on fearlessness, retains pride but replaces "superior to other nations" with acknowledgment of other nations' worthiness. A nation of "healthy chauvinists" would love their homeland while simultaneously acknowledging other homelands to be equally lovable. Daily, however, we see the results of ordinary chauvinism: fear, war, intolerance, and poor communication among ourselves and between nations.

Healthy chauvinism, in turn, reflects near composites. Sometimes the components of near composites are qualitatively different: it is good to be a nearly autonomous man; it is good to be a nearly autonomous woman; together they can form a near composite marriage. Sometimes the components of near composites are quantitatively different: it is good to be a nearly autonomous professional hornist; it is good to be a nearly autonomous non-professional hornist; together we form a near composite of horn players.

When mixtures, compounds, and near composites combine into larger structures, they echo the characteristics of their smallest constituent units, behaving as either dependents or as near autonomies.

Relationships and Horn Sections

THE QUALITY of "mixture" horn sections is produced by chance. Unfortunately, chance usually precludes excellence in horn sections, just as it usually precludes excellence in foods produced from random mixtures of ingredients—even when the individual ingredients are of high quality.

The quality of "compound" sections is more varied than that of "mixture" sections because more permutations are possible in the former than in the latter. Most "compound" horn sections are composed of dependents. These sections tend toward dullness because they lack the interest generated by individuality and idiosyncrasy. They also tend toward fearfulness, and thus they avoid the risk-taking necessary for exciting horn playing. Clearly, "compound" horn sections do not live dangerously with the horn.

Occasionally, however, compounds do contain near autonomies. In such cases, these near autonomies have voluntarily given up elements of their individuality, having perceived that the value of the compound of which they become a part offsets their loss of individuality. For example, a nearly autonomous hornist might choose to adopt new equipment or to alter elements of her or his playing so that she or he may join an eminent orchestra with specific requirements in these areas. Such decisions are formidable and must be made with utmost awareness to ensure that core playing elements are not surrendered. Because compounds of near autonomies are technically "suspensions" (their constituents remain bonded only under specific circumstances), should the above orchestra lose its eminence, it also would lose its nearly autonomous players.

Regardless of their composition, however, "compound" horn sections fight overwhelming odds against achieving excellence. Whatever the quality of their players, the absence of individuality usually produces a commensurate absence of "personality." Worthwhile relationships, including horn sections, embrace rather than fear differences. Not surprisingly, the finest horn sections— almost always "composite" sections—flourish within differences. In composite horn sections, each (nearly autonomous) player is in a composite relationship with the other players. These sections exhibit the most worthwhile qualities of mixtures and compounds: mixtures' retention of each player's individuality, and compounds' bonding. Near composite horn sections arise almost directly from the Big Bang, unobtrusively fit into the present, and easily flow into the future. Composite relationships enable sections to accomplish all of the tasks assigned to them: most composers write both for individuals and for sections. Thus, only composite horn sections can allow their individual and collective talents to blossom.

We have seen that the nature and quality of a horn section are largely products of a web of internal and external relationships. First come the internal self-relationships within each section member that determine whether he or she is nearly autonomous or dependent. Next come the relationships—mixtures, compounds, or composites—among each of the players. Depending on its dominant component, this mélange of relationships produces a horn section that itself behaves either as a dependent or a nearly autonomous entity. The horn section then connects with other entities in an ever-growing context of size and time, similar to the lattice of tonal patterns formed by sounded tones, resultant tones, and overtones.

PRACTICALITIES: PHYSICAL AND PHILOSOPHICAL

The first practicality of a horn section is to constitute itself with appropriate players. Most often, these would be near autonomies. The exceptions are found in orchestras that demand a high degree of conformity. In these cases, dependents usually would be the most suitable and available players, since near autonomies most often choose to be part of mixtures or composites.

Having constituted itself, another important practical decision—sometimes a product of the orchestra's style, sometimes made by the conductor, and sometimes made by the horn section itself—concerns what equipment the section will use. Sometimes the decision is made to require that a specific type or brand of horn be used. Sometimes no decision is necessary because equipment simply is not an issue. If a requirement is adopted, it strongly influences the section through its philosophical and, of course, its technical implications. The arguments in favor of sections playing the same type of instrument, whether by requirement or by choice, include the ease of matching tone qualities and pitch, and the ease of compensating for the quirks common to similar instruments. The key word is "ease." Ironically, while it seems at first to be only a helpful trait, ease often proves ultimately to be negative, producing in horn sections the same predictability and dullness found in some gatherings of like-minded people. The "ease" of using similar equipment, therefore, is sought and valued by some kinds of sections, but not by others. "Mixture" sections of near autonomies choosing voluntarily to play similar instruments derive only limited benefits from the ease thus provided, since the instruments are not the preferred type or brand of each player. "Mixture" sections of dependents, on the other hand, enjoy all of the benefits, but also suffer all of the detriments that go along with the ease of playing similar equipment. Near composite sections simply neither seek nor value the ease provided by playing similar instruments. Their combinations of near autonomies into near composites produce sections so self-motivated and self-assured that their nature is to avoid, as much as possible, mandates imposed from without.

Sections playing similar instruments by genuine choice are more likely to be successful than ones playing similar equipment by requirement. The same inner direction that enables them to make this genuine, technical choice also enables them to make genuine, musical choices, and thus in part to offset some of the dullness inherent in sameness.

Once again, only near autonomies can make the genuine choices that must be based on traits such as application, awareness, fearlessness, and good health. Therefore, a horn section that chooses to play similar equipment must be either a mixture of near autonomies, a compound of near autonomies, or a near composite of near autonomies.

Playing dissimilar equipment can benefit a horn section by enlarging its range of technical and musical resources. These resources can increase a section's variety of sound coloration: one dark-sounding or bright-sounding instrument used imaginatively can change the sound of an entire section; one directional or non-directional sound can change the projection of an entire section. Furthermore, players who choose to play different instruments are usually products of different schools of horn playing. They bring diverse musical ideas from these schools, and their diversity, when transformed into cohesion, adds depth and solidity to a section. Such transformation occurs only in near composite sections that approach diversity through the dual paradigms of mixtures and compounds.

The pinnacle for horn sections is reached by near composite sections playing dissimilar instruments. Only the most enlightened of these sections successfully *require* dissimilar instruments: they are aware of both the potential benefits and the difficulties implied by this mandate, realize that the benefits can be achieved only through great effort, and are willing to make the effort. Without such willingness to find common ground, to teach each other, and sometimes to "agree to disagree," mandated diversity would produce only discord.

Mixture sections, unlike near composite sections, do not necessarily benefit from diversity, because they seek only to retain the individuality of their members, without simultaneously seeking to bond. Their mixture of individualities produces either good or poor sections only through happenstance. Finally, "compound" sections, whether they are composed of nearly autonomous or dependent players, avoid the problems of diversity by the direct expedient of avoiding diversity itself.

A horn section must also choose its philosophical practicalities. Only a section of near autonomies can attend to these important matters, because only near autonomies can make genuine choices. One philosophical practicality regards a section's relationship to the orchestra and whether the section wishes to be part of the overall orchestral texture, or to emphasize its "horn-ness." In horn sections, compounds of dependents or of near autonomies merge or separate according to chance; mixtures of near autonomies usually choose separation from the orchestra; near composites of near autonomies choose either to merge or to emphasize their "horn-ness" based on musical circumstances.

Another philosophical practicality concerns risk-taking, the necessity for which increases as the section's musical aspirations increase. The amount of risk-taking by a section is mostly a product of the relationships among its members. Fearful sections (usually "compound" sections) are often content with safety, and thus do not feel compelled to take risks; fearless sections (generally, mixtures or near composites) strive for artistry and thus feel compelled to take risks.

A third, and controversial, philosophical practicality regards the rewriting of the section's parts, such as dividing passages among several players, reducing doubled parts to one player, and reinforcing lines. The controversy is that it is possibly disrespectful to a composer to rewrite his or her horn part(s). We must remember that our first responsibility is to play, whenever possible, a composer's exact notation. It is inappropriate to rewrite parts that are difficult but playable; we should not rewrite parts only so that we may live *less* dangerously with the horn.

Most composers, like most hornists, are good at what they do, and their music ought not to be rewritten. Good composers take risks just as good hornists do, and the results are usually satisfactory. Difficult passages usually do not indicate ignorance of orchestration. Rather, they are evidence of intelligent—even fearless—orchestration that achieves excitement through the players' overcoming technical hurdles. Gratuitous rewriting of difficult but playable passages, either by dividing, reducing, or reinforcing them, changes the aural design imagined by the composer, and I believe this to be disrespectful.

Rewriting may be justified, nevertheless, when it helps players to "get through the piece," in the infrequent instances of unplayable (not merely difficult) parts. Composers usually allow for hornists' limitations, and we must sometimes adjust to theirs through rewriting. Rewriting must, however, be only a last resort, since the good achieved is necessarily tainted by our (unintentionally) implied disrespect of the composer's wishes.

Contemporary composers do not always object to rewriting. In the paradigm of healthy relationships this is understandable: fine music-making requires a composite of nearly autonomous players, a nearly autonomous conductor, a nearly autonomous hall, a nearly autonomous audience—

and a nearly autonomous composer. Near autonomy, however, does not assure excellence: even less gifted composers may be nearly autonomous and in composite relationships with their interpreters. These composers would tend to be sympathetic both to their *own* technical shortcomings and those of others. On the other hand, when composers are not available for consultation, it is necessary that we make genuine choices regarding the rewriting of their music.

The most common and least controversial aspect of rewriting is to divide passages among several players in order to provide brief respites during very long passages. For example, in the long (and high) first horn solo near the end of the first movement of Shostakovitch's First Symphony, the assistant first horn often plays several of the long notes at the ends of phrases. Like all forms of rewriting, these divisions should be made only when they are unavoidable, and with awareness of their costs. Even when skillfully executed, divisions are audible under close scrutiny—the very degree of scrutiny that we apply to ourselves and hope to receive from our colleagues, conductor, and audience.

For the same reason, we ought not to reduce the forces called for in an orchestration, except when the composer has asked for an impossibility. A reduction usually is made to produce a softer dynamic level, but such "thinning" ought not to be casually undertaken: one horn playing at *piano* does not sound the same as two horns playing together at *pianissimo.* The practice of "thinning" is inadvisable, for instance, at the beginning of Schubert's "Great" C-Major Symphony: although we would achieve the desired dynamic level, the texture and sound imagined by the composer would not be realized.

The issues associated with reinforcing a line for increased volume by adding more horn players are the same as for "thinning." Thus, reinforcing also should be avoided except when a composer has asked for the impossible. Reinforcing a line does indeed raise the dynamic level, but it also changes the texture and the sound quality of the passage. Reinforcing the long passage toward the end of the last movement of Beethoven's "Eroica" Symphony, for example, is an unfortunate practice: three hornists (or four, if the assistant first joins in) easily achieve a loud dynamic level, but produce a sound quality quite different from fewer players achieving, with effort, the same dynamic level.

Finally, we should not rewrite to avoid possible intonational problems. We might be tempted to do so, for example, in the gently echoing section in the last movement of Bach's First Brandenburg Concerto. The issues are the same as with "thinning" and reinforcing of lines: no matter how well-matched they are, either by design or by chance, every player's tone has a unique personality. One horn repeating a passage sounds different from two horns echoing it.

No man—and no orchestra—is an island. Healthy relationships are essential to the best possible music-making, especially in the context of application, awareness, fearlessness, and good health. All of these qualities in turn contribute to the development of our best—our most perfect—selves, and our most perfect music-making.

God is in the details.

—Gustave Flaubert (attrib.)

V

PERFECTION AND PERFECTIONISM

W E HUMANS CANNOT attain perfection. To do so would require resources we simply do not possess, including complete awareness, full autonomy, unlimited intuitive and mechanical skills, boundless time and energy, and so forth. Millions of years ago, the Big Bang sent out multiform and multidirectional streams of energy, and if human perfection were attainable, it would be an unimpeded product of this. From the moment of birth, however, forces such as society, parents, and peers, tend to separate us from our particular, individual (and partially unrealized) energy streams, in terms of which each of us defines "perfection." Therefore, one person's "perfect" is another's "imperfect."

Natural perfection, such as we observe in a crystal, is detailed in form and content, yet it is also direct, there being no obstacles in its path. Likewise, human perfection would be detailed, but indirect, requiring first that we eliminate imperfections such as unawareness, lack of imagination, fear, false ego, and poor health, and then applying awareness, imagination, fearlessness, true ego, and good health to intuitive or learned knowledge of the details of form and content that would comprise perfection. With unlimited resources, we could overcome our imperfections, reunite with our individual energy streams of the Big Bang, and emerge as perfect people and perfect hornists.

PERFECTIONISM

WE HUMANS deal with our imperfections in various ways. At one end of the continuum, some of us feel overwhelmed by imperfections, and we try to dissociate from them, from society, and even from ourselves. At the other end of the spectrum, some of us become "perfectionists"—we set unrealistically high standards, and are displeased with anything less.

Perfectionism rests on foundations ranging from the healthy to the pathological, including artistry, religious beliefs, ignorance, fear, insecurity, and a desire for control. Confronting our imperfections through perfectionism is often as pathological as retreating from them through dissociation. For this reason, perfectionism is usually considered aberrant psychological, spiritual, or physical behavior that is demanding, exhausting, and frustrating.

Nonetheless, I believe that perfectionism can be constructive behavior, but only if it is intermingled with artistry, awareness, imagination, control, fearlessness, good health, belief in the benevolence of the universe, and positive relationships.

There are many paradigms through which we may examine perfectionism. Two such viewpoints include the psychological, that sees perfectionism as a form of co-dependency, and the theological, that sees perfectionism as attempted realignment with the Divine. In these pages, our viewpoint will be pragmatic, considering perfectionism as either destructive or potentially constructive behavior. We will call the first (destructive) type "diffused" perfectionism; it can be practiced by dependents or by near autonomies choosing to do so. We will call the second (constructive) type "specific" perfectionism; it can be practiced only by near autonomies.

"Diffused" and "specific" perfectionism differ from each other essentially. The terminologies are applicable only within each particular situation and within the context of the complete physical and psychological make-up of each individual, including such factors as levels of artistry, awareness, control, imagination, fearlessness, health, expectations, and belief in the goodness of the universe. In other words, one person's "specific" perfectionism is another's "diffused" perfectionism. For example, a nearly autonomous person applying perfectionism to several areas might well be a "specific" perfectionist, whereas a dependent person scattering perfectionism to the same several areas would in all likelihood be a "diffused" perfectionist.

Like a chameleon constantly changing its color, perfectionism causes us constantly to change our definition of "perfection" as our skills for reaching perfection evolve. We are challenged by moving targets, including our individual, evolving definitions of "perfection" and our evolving awareness, sensitivity, fearlessness, and physical abilities. Because it is variable, perfectionism demands understanding of both control (to negotiate our current path toward perfection) and spontaneity (to re-negotiate so that we may accommodate changes in the direction of this path, or in the path itself). We should note that although perfectionism is a flawed product of human behavior, perfectionism's goal—perfection—is a stable, unlimited, and unflawed product of the Big Bang. In addition, perfectionism is an active behavior, demanding a high (and potentially dangerous) degree of physical and emotional application. The eighteenth-century English theologian John Wesley wrote, "Talent is cheap; discipline can cost you your life." A more recent verification of the costs of perfectionism came from Jascha Heifitz, who was approached after a recital by an admirer who exclaimed, "I would give my life to play like that!" To this he replied, "I did."

Society tends to discourage extremes of thought or action, including both types of perfectionism. It often misunderstands perfection, thinking instead of cost, simplicity, size, or popularity. Many writers have expressed themselves on this subject. The contemporary American novelist James Lee Burke, for instance, addressed popularity thus: "If everyone agrees on something, it's probably wrong." Society also often confuses what *is* with what is *possible,* as is evidenced in the saying, "Don't fix it if it ain't broke." "Ain't broke" does not imply "as perfect as possible." Rather, it merely implies "good enough."

"Diffused" Perfectionism

THIS TYPE of perfectionism is indiscriminately applied to every aspect of living—our work, family, relationships, possessions, knowledge, actions, ideas, and thoughts. It is a quest for the impossible. "Diffused" perfectionism can be either a default or a chosen behavior. It is frequently pathological, often arising from un-awareness, fearfulness (mainly, the fear of failure), a lack of understanding of control, and false ego. The "diffused" perfectionism practiced by "dependent" people is perfectionism at its most destructive.

"Diffused" perfectionism produces frustration by causing its practitioners to seek goals so widespread that they make little progress toward reaching any of them. This behavior is also physically destructive: "diffused" perfectionists are never "off duty," and consequently are perpetually overburdened physically, emotionally, and spiritually. "Diffused" perfectionists almost always are "dependent" people: the lack of focus in this type of perfectionism is tailor-made to match with the same qualities we find in "dependency." "Diffused" perfectionism produces in dependent people (who are the very individuals least able to cope with them) feelings of frustration and failure so overwhelming that they can precipitate depression, withdrawal from life, and even suicide.

Nearly autonomous people rarely choose "diffused" perfectionism: they are usually unwilling to scatter their resources so haphazardly. In the rare cases in which near autonomies do choose this type of perfectionism (perhaps they are multi-talented, or are attracted to extraordinary challenges), they choose it with full awareness of its nature, and in possession of many resources necessary to address "diffused" perfectionism's extraordinary challenges. Even then, near autonomies often later change to "specific" perfectionism.

"Specific" Perfectionism

THE SECOND TYPE of perfectionism is perfectionism relatively confined to one or a few areas. Like "diffused" perfectionism, "specific" perfectionism can be either a random behavior of dependent people or a chosen behavior of nearly autonomous ones. Unlike "diffused" perfectionism's quest for the impossible, however, "specific" perfectionism is a quest for the merely quite difficult and improbable. Although the goals of "specific" perfectionism are limited, some of the energy funneled toward them often overflows into other areas—but in the pursuit of excellence, rather than perfection. This explains why, for instance, a "specific" perfectionist horn player often excels in other areas of her or his life.

Because "specific" perfectionism's goal or goals are limited, it is possible for this type of perfectionist to go "off duty" when not actively engaged in the targeted challenge. But this is only a possibility: a dependent "specific" perfectionist cannot choose to be "on duty" or "off duty," and is usually "on the job," whereas a nearly autonomous "specific" perfectionist can choose whether or not to take time away from her or his perfectionism. As a random behavior of a dependent person, "specific" perfectionism has the same liabilities as "diffused" perfectionism, although to a lesser extent. On the other hand, as the chosen behavior of a nearly autonomous person, "specific" perfectionism can be a constructive, even desirable, behavior.

Nearly Autonomous "Specific" Perfectionism

HEALTHY "SPECIFIC" PERFECTIONISM is built on facets of near autonomy, such as the understanding of control, the ability to make and the knowledge to implement genuine choices, and the ability to enter into composite relationships. Horn players who are nearly autonomous "specific" perfectionists more often attain near-perfection than other kinds of perfectionist horn players. Being nearly autonomous, they are guided by their most aware inner voices, urging them toward perfection. Nearly autonomous "specific" perfectionists choose an area or areas that are appropriate for their perfectionism. They also determine what is "appropriate," and do not allow others to dissuade them from their determinations— or their determination. These carefully chosen areas naturally provide much of the energy necessary to sustain the "specific" perfectionists on their journeys toward the unattainable. (They also provide for us yet another parallel to our sun simultaneously burning and generating fuel.)

The "specific" perfectionism of near autonomies is based on a high degree of awareness. Awareness, as well as belief and trust in the benevolence of the universe, promotes fearlessness and makes risk-taking possible. Awareness also makes possible acceptance of the inevitable missteps inherent in the journey toward perfection: American Yale law professor Edward John Phelps (1822–1900) wrote that "The man who makes no mistakes does not usually make anything."

"Specific" perfectionism also is predicated on healthy involvement with work. It is imperative that "specific" perfectionists avoid "identifying" with and "losing" themselves in their work. As we discussed in Chapter Four, "identification" is not a type of relationship. Rather it is a *behavior* that produces conditions of engulfment by inanimate objects or experiences. "Identifying" with other entities, be they our work, our ideas, other people, flowers, beautiful sunsets, catastrophes, or symphonies, causes us to lose whatever may be our degrees of autonomy, and, in effect, causes us to "become" that other entity. For example, if people approve of stories we tell and we identify too closely with these stories, we interpret this praise as approval of *us:* we *are* the stories. If people admire our clothing and we identify with it, we interpret this as admiration of *us:* we *are* the clothing. "Identifying" with anything precludes composite relationships with the objects of the identification, and negates the individuality of both the human beings and of the things or experiences with which they identify.

On the other hand, when we are in near composite relationships with, for example, beautiful sunsets, the "mixture" part of the relationships allows us to retain our individualities and objectivities, while the "compound" part of the relationships allows us to react strongly to the beautiful skies. As horn players, we must immerse ourselves in our playing without identifying with it. Of course, our playing should represent and reflect us, but we must not *be* our playing.

Nearly autonomous "specific" perfectionists realize that their efforts toward inner perfection must be made before, or at least simultaneously with, their efforts toward outer perfection. Because both targets are unachievable, all perfectionists, including nearly autonomous ones, occasionally feel like frauds. In near autonomies, these feelings are internally generated rather than "other-generated," and result from conflicts among their inner voices, some of which remain silent out of ignorance, fear, indolence, or apathy, while others demand perfection. (Unlike in a complete autonomy, both positive and negative "voices" vie for the floor in a near autonomy.)

Even nearly autonomous "specific" perfectionists dart in and out of territories that deny them permanent visas. These feelings can be assuaged by taking a cue from folk wisdom and perceiving their glasses as half full rather than as half empty, standing on the solid knowledge of what they can produce rather than sinking into the abyss of what they cannot. Nearly autonomous "specific" perfectionists should remember that their efforts do not guarantee that they will reach either their inner or outer goals. Ironically, "diffused" perfectionists, or even dependent non-perfectionists possessing strong innate talent, may occasionally reach higher levels of playing, and enjoy more outer success, than their less talented, nearly autonomous, "specific" perfectionist colleagues.

Nearly autonomous "specific" perfectionists are concerned with their processes, and consider their goals to be by-products of these processes. For this reason, they are less frustrated by not reaching their outer goals than their "diffused" perfectionist colleagues. On the other hand, nearly autonomous "specific" perfectionists are more frustrated by internal imperfections such as incomplete awareness, than are their "diffused"perfectionist colleagues.

Even "specific" perfectionism (with its limited goals) as practiced by near autonomies (with their vast resources) is a difficult path. Nearly autonomous "specific" perfectionists know to expect society neither to agree with their goals, nor to reward their efforts to attain them. The primary rewards of these perfectionists are self-affirmation and the excitement of confronting their chosen challenges.

"Specific" perfectionism, however, is not suitable for all nearly autonomous hornists. Prior to adopting "specific" perfectionism, such players should carefully choose how they wish to balance their individual well-being (including, for instance, their psychological ease) with society's interests (including, for example, its culture). Nearly autonomous horn players who desire personal well-being avoid both types of perfectionism, choosing instead to be in mixture relationships with society, preferring the ease provided by such relationships (which require very little expenditure of effort) rather than the difficulties and dangers of "specific" perfectionism. On the other hand, nearly autonomous players who desire involvement with society as well as the respite available because of the possibility of being "off duty" sometimes, choose the rigors of "specific" perfectionism in composite relationships with society. In choosing appropriate balances between individual well-being and the needs of society, few "specific" perfectionists choose extreme positions.

Achieving near autonomy and "specific" perfectionism within composite relationships are worthy and difficult goals. But, as we have seen, they can be accomplished. Bob Edwards, host of National Public Radio's "Morning Edition," recently published *Fridays with Red: A Radio Friendship,* recounting his friendship with baseball announcer (and lay Episcopal church reader) Red Barber. It includes this passage:

A trip to Spain in 1953 gave him one of his best sermons. It was titled "Mira detrás de la capa," or "Look Behind the Cape." In the sermon, Red describes a bullfight, and he does not spare one gory detail. He acknowledges his bias towards the bull and says he kept trying to send the bull a message by mental telepathy: "Look behind the cape." Behind that moving cape is the sword. The lesson is that we should know our real enemy. It's not the cape. It's what is behind the cape. I love that one.

Behind the cape of our imperfect playing hide our real enemies: unawareness, fear, ignorance, lack of vision, defensiveness, fearfulness, poor health, and more. Although these foes cannot be completely vanquished, they can be subdued by following the difficult paths that lead toward artistry, fearlessness, near autonomy, near composite relationships and "specific" perfectionism—by living dangerously with the horn.

BIBLIOGRAPHY

CHAPTER 1

Abbott, Charles David. *Howard Pyle: A Chronicle*. New York: Harper, 1925.

Allen, Henry. "America the Bummed. We are Afraid, Guilty, Whiny, and Fatigued. We are Mired in Malaise. We've Fallen and We Can't Get Up." *Newsday,* 4 December 1990, 82 (2).

Armer, Laura Adams. *Dark Circle of Branches*. New York: Longman, Green, 1933.

Bradbury, Ray. *Zen and the Art of Writing: Essays on Creativity*. Santa Barbara, Calif.: Capra Press, 1973.

Crisp, Quentin. *The Wit and Wisdom of Quentin Crisp*. Edited and compiled by Guy Kettelhack. New York: Harper and Row, 1984.

Castaneda, Carlos. *The Teachings of Don Juan: A Yaqui Way of Knowledge*. Berkeley: University of California Press, 1968.

Dillard, Annie. *The Writing Life*. New York: HarperCollins, 1989.

Goldberg, Natalie. *Writing Down the Bones: Freeing the Writer Within*. Boston: Shambhala Publications, 1986.

Gould, Stephen Jay. *The Flamingo's Smile: Reflections in Natural History*. New York: W. W. Norton, 1985.

Lindsey, David L. *In the Lake of the Moon*. New York: Simon & Schuster, 1988.

Maclean, Norman. *A River Runs Through It and Other Stories*. Chicago: University of Chicago Press, 1976.

Maxym, Stephen. "The Technique of Breathing for Wind Instruments." *Woodwind Magazine* 5 (December 1952): 4, 9, 14; 5 (January 1953): 4, 11; 5 (February 1953): 5, 9, 14; 5 (March 1953): 8, 14, 15; 5 (April 1953): 6, 9, 14.

Melville, Herman. *Moby-Dick*. Edited by Harrison Hayford and Herschel Parker. New York: W. W. Norton, 1967.

Miller, Henry. *The Air-Conditioned Nightmare*. New York: New Directions Publishing Corp., 1945.

Muktananda, Swami. *The Perfect Relationship.* South Fallsburg, N.Y.: SYDA Foundation, 1980.

Nash, Ogden. *Verses from 1929.* New York: Little, Brown & Co., 1940.

CHAPTER 2

Farkas, Philip. *The Art of French Horn Playing.* Evanston, Ill.: Summy–Birchard, 1956.

Hillerman, Tony. *Sacred Clowns.* New York: HarperCollins,1993.

Kanigel, Robert. *The Man Who Knew Infinity: A Life of the Genius Ramanujan.* New York: Simon & Schuster, Scribner, 1991.

Maclean, Norman. *A River Runs Through It and Other Stories.* Chicago: University of Chicago Press, 1976.

————. *Young Men and Fire: A True Story of the Mann Gulch Fire.* Chicago: University of Chicago Press, 1992.

Trungpa, Chogyam. *Shambhala: The Sacred Path of the Warrior.* Boston: Shambhala Publications, 1984.

CHAPTER 3

Carlson, Richard, and Benjamin Shield, eds. *Healers on Healing.* With a Foreword by W. Brough Joy, M.D. Los Angeles: Putnam Publishing Group, Jeremy P. Tarcher, Inc., 1989.

CHAPTER 4

Lawrence, David Herbert. *The Complete Poems of D. H. Lawrence.* Edited by V. de Sola Pinto, and F. W. Roberts. New York: Viking Penguin, 1964.

CHAPTER 5

Edwards, Bob. *Fridays with Red; A Radio Friendship.* New York: Simon & Schuster, 1993.

RECOMMENDED ADDITIONAL READING

Albee, Edward. *The Zoo Story.* New York: New American Library, 1959.

A Barefoot Doctor's Manual; The American Translation of the Official Chinese Paramedical Manual. Philadelphia: Running Press, 1977.

Bernstein, Leonard. *The Joy of Music.* New York: Simon & Schuster, 1959.

Berry, Wallace. *Form in Music.* Englewood Cliffs, N. J.: Prentice–Hall, Inc., 1966.

Berv, Harry. *A Creative Appproach to the French Horn.* Bryn Mawr, Penn.: Theodore Presser Co., 1977.

Bristol, Claude M. *The Magic of Believing.* Englewood Cliffs, N.J.: Prentice–Hall, Inc., 1948.

Bynner, Witter, trans. *The Way of Life According to Lao-Tzu.* New York: Berkley Publishing Group, 1944.

Ciardi, John. *How Does a Poem Mean?* Boston: Houghton Mifflin, 1959.

Donden, Yeshi. *Health Through Balance: An Introduction to Tibetan Medicine.* Edited by Jeffrey Hopkins; Translated by Jeffrey Hopkins, Lobsang Rabgay, and Alan Wallace. Ithaca, N.Y.: Snow Lion Publications, 1986.

Eisenberg, David, M. D. *Encounters with Qi: Exploring Chinese Medicine.* With a foreword by Herbert Benson, M. D. New York: W. W. Norton, 1985.

Frank, Jerome David. *Persuasion and Healing: A Comparative Study of Psychotherapy.* Rev. ed. New York: Schocken Books, 1973.

Gilligan, Carol. *In a Different Voice.* Cambridge: Harvard University Press, 1982.

Goetchius, Percy. *The Homophonic Forms of Musical Composition.* New York: Edwin F. Kalmus, 1897.

Gurdjieff, Georges Ivanovitch. *Meetings with Remarkable Men.* Translated by A. R. Orage. New York: Dutton, 1963.

Hayakawa, Samuel Ichiye. *Language in Thought and Action.* New York: Harcourt Brace Jovanovich, 1978.

Herrigel, Eugen. *Zen: Including Zen in the Art of Archery.* With an introduction by D. T. Suzuki. New York: McGraw–Hill Book Co., 1964.

Humphrey, Doris. *The Art of Making Dances.* New York: Grove Press, 1959.

Kaptchuk, Ted J. *The Web That Has No Weaver: Understanding Chinese Medicine.* New York: Congdon and Weed, 1983.

Klausner, Samuel Z., ed. *Why Man Takes Chances.* New York: Doubleday Anchor, 1968.

Kleist, Heinrich von. *The Marquis of O–And Other Stories.* Translated by David Luke and Nigel Reeves. New York: Penguin, 1978.

Koestler, Arthur. *The Act of Creation: A Study of the Conscious and Unconscious in Science and Art.* New York: Dell Publishing Co., 1964.

Kostka, Stefan. *Materials and Techniques of Twentieth Century Music.* Englewood Cliffs, N. J.: Prentice–Hall, 1990.

Leuba, Christopher. *A Study of Musical Intonation.* Minneapolis: Prospect Publications, 1962.

Muktananda, Swami. *Where are You Going?* Ganeshpuri, India: Gurudev Siddha Peeth, 1981.

Ouspensky, Peter Demianovich. *In Search of The Miraculous: Fragments of an Unknown Teaching.* New York: Harcourt, Brace and Co., 1949.

Payer, Lynn. *Disease-Mongers: How Doctors, Drug Companies, and Insurers Are Making You Feel Sick.* New York: John Wiley and Sons, 1992.

————. *Medicine and Culture: Varieties in Treatment in the United States, England, West Germany, and France.* New York: Henry Holt and Co., 1988.

Peel, Robert. *Spiritual Healing in a Scientific Age.* San Francisco: Harper and Row, 1987.

Pleasants, Henry. *The Agony of Modern Music.* New York: Simon &

Schuster, 1955.

Post, Laurens van der. *A Mantis Carol.* New York: William Morrow and Co., 1975.

Rama, Swami, Rudolph Ballentine, M.D., and Alan Hymes, M.D. *Science of Breath.* Honesdale, Penn.: Himalayan Institute, 1979.

Raymo, Chet. *The Virgin and the Mousetrap: Essays in Search of the Soul of Science.* New York: Viking, 1991.

Ristad, Eloise. *A Soprano on Her Head: Right-side-up Reflections on Life and Other Performances.* Moab, Utah: Real People Press, 1982.

Rumi, Mevlana Jelaluddin. *Unseen Rain: Quatrains of Rumi.* Translated by John Moyne and Coleman Barks. Putney, Vt.: Threshold Books, 1986.

Saint-Exupéry, Antoine de. *The Little Prince.* Translated by Katherine Woods. New York: Harcourt, Brace and World, 1943.

Salinger, Jerome David. *Franny and Zooey.* New York: Little, Brown and Co., 1955.

Schuller Gunther. *Studies for Unaccompanied Horn.* New York: Oxford University Press, 1962.

Selzer, Richard. *Mortal Lessons.* New York: Simon & Schuster, 1974.

Shawn, W. and A. Gregory. *My Dinner with André.* New York: Grove Press, 1981.

Smith, Ann W. *Overcoming Perfectionism: The Key to a Balanced Recovery.* Deerfield Beach, Fla.: Health Communications, Inc., 1990.

Spencer, Peter, and Peter M. Temko. *The Study of Form in Music.* Englewood Cliffs, N. J.: Prentice–Hall, 1990.

Sullivan, J. W. N. *Beethoven: His Spiritual Development.* New York: New American Library 1949.

Thomas, Lewis. *The Fragile Species: Notes of a Biology Watcher.* Toronto: Charles Scribner's Sons, 1974.

———. *The Lives of a Cell.* New York: Bantam Books, 1974.

von Ditfurth, Hoimar. Translated by Jan van Heurck. *Children of the*

Universe. New York: Atheneum Publishers, 1974.

Walker, Brian. *Hua Hu Ching: The Unknown Teachings of Lao-Tzu.* San Francisco: Harper, 1992.

Watts, Alan W. *The Wisdom of Insecurity.* New York: Pantheon, 1951.

Woodman, Marion. *Addiction to Perfection: The Still Unravished Bride.* Toronto: Inner City Books, 1982.

INDEX